COMMON CORE

SKILLS & STRATEGIES FOR READING

Level 8

SADDLEBACK
EDUCATIONAL PUBLISHING

COMMON CORE

SKILLS & STRATEGIES FOR READING

Level 3

Level 4

Level 5

Level 6

Level 7

Level 8

SADDLEBACK
EDUCATIONAL PUBLISHING
www.sdlback.com

© 2002, 2011, 2013 by Saddleback Educational Publishing

ISBN-13: 978-1-62250-059-8
ISBN-10: 1-62250-059-8
eBook: 978-1-61247-717-6

Printed in the United States of America

17 16 15 14 13   1 2 3 4 5

Table of Contents
Skills

Welcome to
Common Core Skills & Strategies for Reading

About This Series

The Common Core State Standards (CCSS) provide a consistent, clear understanding of what students are expected to learn. Aligning each lesson in these six Common Core titles to the CCSS ensures that students are being taught and assessed on what they are expected to learn and know. The alignment helps educators think critically about their curriculum, instruction, and assessments as they work to ensure that their students meet the rigorous new standards.

Beginning with foundational skills, the activities teach students what they need to learn. The alignments offer a progressive development of reading comprehension skills so that students advancing through the levels are able to gain more from whatever they read. Each title includes a table of contents, a CCSS alignment chart, 130 reproducible lessons individually aligned to the CCSS (each lesson contains a discrete alignment at the bottom of the page), a scope and sequence chart, and an answer key.

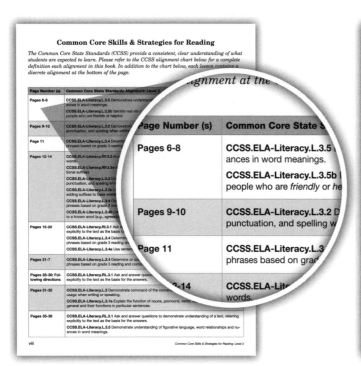

CCSS Alignment Chart

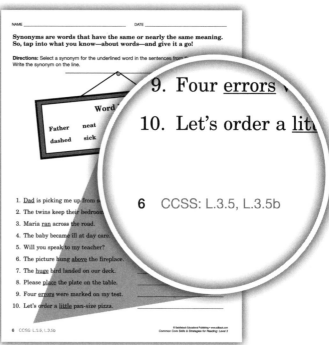

Discrete Alignment on Each Page

About This Book

Common Core Skills and Strategies for Reading is designed to reinforce and extend the reading skills of your students. The fun, high-interest fiction and nonfiction selections will spark the interest of even your most reluctant reader. The book offers your students a variety of reading opportunities—reading for pleasure, reading to gather information, and reading to perform a task. Each page offers the opportunity for the student to apply one of the strategies to the reading selection, which is linked to a relevant comprehension skill activity.

Each book includes a CD, which contains a complete electronic version of the reproducible as an "Unlocked PDF." Unlocked PDFs allow users to copy/paste text and certain images for posting, emailing, projecting on a whiteboard, and more.

Choosing Instructional Approaches

You can use the pages in this book for independent reinforcement or extension, whole group lessons, pairs, or small cooperative groups rotating through an established reading learning center. You may choose to place the activities in a center and reproduce the answer key for self-checking. To ensure the utmost flexibility, the process for managing this is left entirely up to you because you know what works best in your classroom.

Assessment

Assessment and evaluation of student understanding and ability is an ongoing process. A variety of methods and strategies should be used to ensure that the student is being assessed and evaluated in a fair and comprehensive manner. Always keep in mind that the assessment should take into consideration the opportunities the student had to learn the information and practice the skills presented. The strategies for assessment are left for you to determine and are dependent on your students and your particular instructional plan. You will find a Scope and Sequence Chart at the back of this book to assist you as you develop your assessment plan.

Common Core Skills & Strategies for Reading

The Common Core State Standards (CCSS) provide a consistent, clear understanding of what students are expected to learn. Please refer to the CCSS alignment chart below for a complete definition each alignment in this book. In addition to the chart below, each lesson contains a discrete alignment at the bottom of the page.

Page Number (s)	Common Core State Standards Alignment: Level 8
Pages 2-8	**CCSS.ELA-Literacy.L.8.4** Determine or clarify the meaning of unknown and multiple-meaning words or phrases based on grade 8 reading and content, choosing flexibly from a range of strategies. **CCSS.ELA-Literacy.L.8.4b** Use common, grade-appropriate Greek or Latin affixes and roots as clues to the meaning of a word (e.g., *precede, recede, secede*).
Page 9	**CCCSS.ELA-Literacy.L.8.1** Demonstrate command of the conventions of standard English grammar and usage when writing or speaking.
Pages 10-18	**CCSS.ELA-Literacy.L.8.4** Determine or clarify the meaning of unknown and multiple-meaning words or phrases based on grade 8 reading and content, choosing flexibly from a range of strategies. **CCSS.ELA-Literacy.L.8.4a** Use context (e.g., the overall meaning of a sentence or paragraph; a word's position or function in a sentence) as a clue to the meaning of a word or phrase.
Page 19	**CCSS.ELA-Literacy.W.8.2d** Use precise language and domain-specific vocabulary to inform about or explain the topic.
Page 20	**CCSS.ELA-Literacy.L.8.4d** Verify the preliminary determination of the meaning of a word or phrase (e.g., by checking the inferred meaning in context or in a dictionary).
Pages 21-26	**CCSS.ELA-Literacy.L.8.5** Demonstrate understanding of figurative language, word relationships, and nuances in word meanings. **CCSS.ELA-Literacy.L.8.5b** Use the relationship between particular words to better understand each of the words.
Pages 27-29	**CCSS.ELA-Literacy.L.8.4** Determine or clarify the meaning of unknown and multiple-meaning words or phrases based on grade 8 reading and content, choosing flexibly from a range of strategies.
Pages 30-31	**CCSS.ELA-Literacy.L.8.4d** Verify the preliminary determination of the meaning of a word or phrase (e.g., by checking the inferred meaning in context or in a dictionary). **CCSS.ELA-Literacy.L.8.1** Demonstrate command of the conventions of standard English grammar and usage when writing or speaking.
Pages 32-37	**CCSS.ELA-Literacy.L.8.5** Demonstrate understanding of figurative language, word relationships, and nuances in word meanings. **CCSS.ELA-Literacy.L.8.5b** Use the relationship between particular words to better understand each of the words. **CCSS.ELA-Literacy.L.8.5c** Distinguish among the connotations (associations) of words with similar denotations (definitions) (e.g., *bullheaded, willful, firm, persistent, resolute*).
Page 38	**CCSS.ELA-Literacy.L.8.1** Demonstrate command of the conventions of standard English grammar and usage when writing or speaking. **CCSS.ELA-Literacy.L.8.4a** Use context (e.g., the overall meaning of a sentence or paragraph; a word's position or function in a sentence) as a clue to the meaning of a word or phrase. **CCSS.ELA-Literacy.L.8.6** Acquire and use accurately grade-appropriate general academic and domain-specific words and phrases; gather vocabulary knowledge when considering a word or phrase important to comprehension or expression.

Page Number (s)	Common Core State Standards Alignment: Level 8
Page 39	**CCSS.ELA-Literacy.L.8.4d** Verify the preliminary determination of the meaning of a word or phrase (e.g., by checking the inferred meaning in context or in a dictionary).
Page 40	**CCSS.ELA-Literacy.W.8.2c** Use appropriate and varied transitions to create cohesion and clarify the relationships among ideas and concepts.
Page 41	**CCSS.ELA-Literacy.L.8.2** Demonstrate command of the conventions of standard English capitalization, punctuation, and spelling when writing.
Page 42	**CCSS.ELA-Literacy.RH.6-8.2** Determine the central ideas or information of a primary or secondary source; provide an accurate summary of the source distinct from prior knowledge or opinions. **CCSS.ELA-Literacy.WHST.6-8.9** Draw evidence from informational texts to support analysis reflection, and research.
Page 43	**CCSS.ELA-Literacy.RL.8.2** Determine a theme or central idea of a text and analyze its development over the course of the text, including its relationship to the characters, setting, and plot; provide an objective summary of the text.
Page 44	**CCSS.ELA-Literacy.W.8.2b** Develop the topic with relevant, well-chosen facts, definitions, concrete details, quotations, or other information and examples. **CCSS.ELA-Literacy.W.8.2d** Use precise language and domain-specific vocabulary to inform about or explain the topic. **CCSS.ELA-Literacy.W.8.2e** Establish and maintain a formal style.
Pages 45-46	**CCSS.ELA-Literacy.RL.8.1** Cite the textual evidence that most strongly supports an analysis of what the text says explicitly as well as inferences drawn from the text.
Pages 47-48	**CCSS.ELA-Literacy.L.8.2** Demonstrate command of the conventions of standard English capitalization, punctuation, and spelling when writing. **CCSS.ELA-Literacy.L.8.2c** Spell correctly.
Page 49	**CCSS.ELA-Literacy.L.8.5** Demonstrate understanding of figurative language, word relationships, and nuances in word meanings. **CCSS.ELA-Literacy.L.8.5b** Use the relationship between particular words to better understand each of the words.
Page 50	**CCSS.ELA-Literacy.RST.6-8.8** Distinguish among facts, reasoned judgment based on research findings, and speculation in a text. **CCSS.ELA-Literacy.L.8.6** Acquire and use accurately grade-appropriate general academic and domain-specific words and phrases; gather vocabulary knowledge when considering a word or phrase important to comprehension or expression.
Pages 51-53	**CCSS.ELA-Literacy.L.8.5** Demonstrate understanding of figurative language, word relationships, and nuances in word meanings. **CCSS.ELA-Literacy.L.8.5b** Use the relationship between particular words to better understand each of the words. **CCSS.ELA-Literacy.L.8.5c** Distinguish among the connotations (associations) of words with similar denotations (definitions) (e.g., *bullheaded, willful, firm, persistent, resolute*).
Pages 54-55	**CCSS.ELA-Literacy.RL.8.1** Cite the textual evidence that most strongly supports an analysis of what the text says explicitly as well as inferences drawn from the text. **CCSS.ELA-Literacy.RL.8.4** Determine the meaning of words and phrases as they are used in a text, including figurative and connotative meanings; analyze the impact of specific word choices on meaning and tone, including analogies or allusions to other texts.

Page Number (s)	Common Core State Standards Alignment: Level 8
Page 56	CCSS.ELA-Literacy.RST.6-8.2 Determine the central ideas or conclusions of a text; provide an accurate summary of the text distinct from prior knowledge or opinions.
Page 57	CCSS.ELA-Literacy.RH.6-8.2 Determine the central ideas or information of a primary or secondary source; provide an accurate summary of the source distinct from prior knowledge or opinions.
Page 58	CCSS.ELA-Literacy.RST.6-8.2 Determine the central ideas or conclusions of a text; provide an accurate summary of the text distinct from prior knowledge or opinions.

CCSS.ELA-Literacy.RST.6-8.4 Determine the meaning of symbols, key terms, and other domain-specific words and phrases as they are used in a specific scientific or technical context relevant to grades 6–8 texts and topics.

CCSS.ELA-Literacy.RST.6-8.8 Distinguish among facts, reasoned judgment based on research findings, and speculation in a text. |
| Pages 59-60 | CCSS.ELA-Literacy.RL.8.1 Cite the textual evidence that most strongly supports an analysis of what the text says explicitly as well as inferences drawn from the text.

CCSS.ELA-Literacy.RL.8.3 Analyze how particular lines of dialogue or incidents in a story or drama propel the action, reveal aspects of a character, or provoke a decision. |
| Pages 61-62 | CCSS.ELA-Literacy.RI.8.8 Delineate and evaluate the argument and specific claims in a text, assessing whether the reasoning is sound and the evidence is relevant and sufficient; recognize when irrelevant evidence is introduced.

CCSS.ELA-Literacy.W.8.2 Write informative/explanatory texts to examine a topic and convey ideas, concepts, and information through the selection, organization, and analysis of relevant content.

CCSS.ELA-Literacy.W.8.2b Develop the topic with relevant, well-chosen facts, definitions, concrete details, quotations, or other information and examples.

CCSS.ELA-Literacy.W.8.2c Use appropriate and varied transitions to create cohesion and clarify the relationships among ideas and concepts.

CCSS.ELA-Literacy.W.8.2d Use precise language and domain-specific vocabulary to inform about or explain the topic.

CCSS.ELA-Literacy.W.8.2e Establish and maintain a formal style.

CCSS.ELA-Literacy.W.8.2f Provide a concluding statement or section that follows from and supports the information or explanation presented. |
| Page 63 | CCSS.ELA-Literacy.RH.6-8.7 Integrate visual information (e.g., in charts, graphs, photographs, videos, or maps) with other information in print and digital texts. |
| Pages 64-67 | CCSS.ELA-Literacy.RL.8.1 Cite the textual evidence that most strongly supports an analysis of what the text says explicitly as well as inferences drawn from the text. |
| Page 68 | CCSS.ELA-Literacy.L.8.5 Demonstrate understanding of figurative language, word relationships, and nuances in word meanings.

CCSS.ELA-Literacy.L.8.5a Interpret figures of speech (e.g. verbal irony, puns) in context |
| Page 69 | CCSS.ELA-Literacy.L.8.5 Demonstrate understanding of figurative language, word relationships, and nuances in word meanings.

CCSS.ELA-Literacy.L.8.5b Use the relationship between particular words to better understand each of the words.

CCSS.ELA-Literacy.W.8.1 Write arguments to support claims with clear reasons and relevant evidence. |
| Page 70 | CCSS.ELA-Literacy.RH.6-8.1 Cite specific textual evidence to support analysis of primary and secondary sources. |

Page Number (s)	Common Core State Standards Alignment: Level 8
Page 71	**CCSS.ELA-Literacy.RH.6-8.1** Cite specific textual evidence to support analysis of primary and secondary sources. **CCSS.ELA-Literacy.RH.6-8.4** Determine the meaning of words and phrases as they are used in a text, including vocabulary specific to domains related to history/social studies. **CCSS.ELA-Literacy.WHST.6-8.2b** Develop the topic with relevant, well-chosen facts, definitions, concrete details, quotations, or other information and examples.
Page 72	**CCSS.ELA-Literacy.RST.6-8.1** Cite specific textual evidence to support analysis of science and technical texts. **CCSS.ELA-Literacy.WHST.6-8.2d** Use precise language and domain-specific vocabulary to inform about or explain the topic. **CCSS.ELA-Literacy.W.8.9** Draw evidence from literary or informational texts to support analysis, reflection, and research.
Pages 73-77	**CCSS.ELA-Literacy.L.8.5** Demonstrate understanding of figurative language, word relationships, and nuances in word meanings. **CCSS.ELA-Literacy.L.8.5a** Interpret figures of speech (e.g. verbal irony, puns) in context **CCSS.ELA-Literacy.L.8.6** Acquire and use accurately grade-appropriate general academic and domain-specific words and phrases; gather vocabulary knowledge when considering a word or phrase important to comprehension or expression.
Pages 78-80	**CCSS.ELA-Literacy.RI.8.8** Delineate and evaluate the argument and specific claims in a text, assessing whether the reasoning is sound and the evidence is relevant and sufficient; recognize when irrelevant evidence is introduced. **CCSS.ELA-Literacy.L.8.5** Demonstrate understanding of figurative language, word relationships, and nuances in word meanings. **CCSS.ELA-Literacy.L.8.6** Acquire and use accurately grade-appropriate general academic and domain-specific words and phrases; gather vocabulary knowledge when considering a word or phrase important to comprehension or expression.
Page 81	**CCSS.ELA-Literacy.RST.6-8.2** Determine the central ideas or conclusions of a text; provide an accurate summary of the text distinct from prior knowledge or opinions. **CCSS.ELA-Literacy.WHST.6-8.8** Gather relevant information from multiple print and digital sources, using search terms effectively; assess the credibility and accuracy of each source; and quote or paraphrase the data and conclusions of others while avoiding plagiarism and following a standard format for citation.
Page 82	**CCSS.ELA-Literacy.RL.8.2** Determine a theme or central idea of a text and analyze its development over the course of the text, including its relationship to the characters, setting, and plot; provide an objective summary of the text. **CCSS.ELA-Literacy.W.8.4** Produce clear and coherent writing in which the development, organization, and style are appropriate to task, purpose, and audience.
Page 83	**CCSS.ELA-Literacy.RL.8.2** Determine a theme or central idea of a text and analyze its development over the course of the text, including its relationship to the characters, setting, and plot; provide an objective summary of the text. **CCSS.ELA-Literacy.W.8.4** Produce clear and coherent writing in which the development, organization, and style are appropriate to task, purpose, and audience. (Grade-specific expectations for writing types are defined in standards 1–3 above **CCSS.ELA-Literacy.SL.8.1** Engage effectively in a range of collaborative discussions (one-on-one, in groups, and teacher-led) with diverse partners on grade 8 topics, texts, and issues, building on others' ideas and expressing their own clearly.
Page 84	**CCSS.ELA-Literacy.RL.8.1** Cite the textual evidence that most strongly supports an analysis of what the text says explicitly as well as inferences drawn from the text.

Page Number (s)	Common Core State Standards Alignment: Level 8
Page 85	**CCSS.ELA-Literacy.RL.8.6** Analyze how differences in the points of view of the characters and the audience or reader (e.g., created through the use of dramatic irony) create such effects as suspense or humor. **CCSS.ELA-Literacy.L.8.6** Acquire and use accurately grade-appropriate general academic and domain-specific words and phrases; gather vocabulary knowledge when considering a word or phrase important to comprehension or expression.
Page 86	**CCSS.ELA-Literacy.W.8.3a** Engage and orient the reader by establishing a context and point of view and introducing a narrator and/or characters; organize an event sequence that unfolds naturally and logically.
Pages 87-88	**CCSS.ELA-Literacy.L.8.4** Determine or clarify the meaning of unknown and multiple-meaning words or phrases based on grade 8 reading and content, choosing flexibly from a range of strategies **CCSS.ELA-Literacy.L.8.4d** Verify the preliminary determination of the meaning of a word or phrase (e.g., by checking the inferred meaning in context or in a dictionary).
Pages 89-90	**CCSS.ELA-Literacy.RL.8.2** Determine a theme or central idea of a text and analyze its development over the course of the text, including its relationship to the characters, setting, and plot; provide an objective summary of the text.
Page 91	**CCSS.ELA-Literacy.W.8.3d** Use precise words and phrases, relevant descriptive
Page 92	**CCSS.ELA-Literacy.L.8.6** Acquire and use accurately grade-appropriate general academic and domain-specific words and phrases; gather vocabulary knowledge when considering a word or phrase important to comprehension or expression.
Page 93-94	**CCSS.ELA-Literacy.RL.8.2** Determine a theme or central idea of a text and analyze its development over the course of the text, including its relationship to the characters, setting, and plot; provide an objective summary of the text. **CCSS.ELA-Literacy.RL.8.3** Analyze how particular lines of dialogue or incidents in a story or drama propel the action, reveal aspects of a character, or provoke a decision.
Page 95	**CCSS.ELA-Literacy.W.8.3a** Engage and orient the reader by establishing a context and point of view and introducing a narrator and/or characters; organize an event sequence that unfolds naturally and logically.
Pages 96-97	**CCSS.ELA-Literacy.RL.8.1** Cite the textual evidence that most strongly supports an analysis of what the text says explicitly as well as inferences drawn from the text.
Page 98	**CCSS.ELA-Literacy.RL.8.4** Determine the meaning of words and phrases as they are used in a text, including figurative and connotative meanings; analyze the impact of specific word choices on meaning and tone, including analogies or allusions to other texts.
Page 99	**CCSS.ELA-Literacy.RL.8.3** Analyze how particular lines of dialogue or incidents in a story or drama propel the action, reveal aspects of a character, or provoke a decision. **CCSS.ELA-Literacy.RL.8.5** Compare and contrast the structure of two or more texts and analyze how the differing structure of each text contributes to its meaning and style.
Page 100	**CCSS.ELA-Literacy.RL.8.6** Analyze how differences in the points of view of the characters and the audience or reader (e.g., created through the use of dramatic irony) create such effects as suspense or humor.
Pages 101-102	CCSS.ELA-Literacy.W.8.3a Engage and orient the reader by establishing a context and point of view and introducing a narrator and/or characters; organize an event sequence that unfolds naturally and logically. CCSS.ELA-Literacy.RL.8.6 Analyze how differences in the points of view of the characters and the audience.

Page Number (s)	Common Core State Standards Alignment: Level 8
Page 103	**CCSS.ELA-Literacy.RL.8.1** Cite the textual evidence that most strongly supports an analysis of what the text says explicitly as well as inferences drawn from the text. **CCSS.ELA-Literacy.RL.8.3** Analyze how particular lines of dialogue or incidents in a story or drama propel the action, reveal aspects of a character, or provoke a decision.
Pages 104-106	**CCSS.ELA-Literacy.RI.8.6** Determine an author's point of view or purpose in a text and analyze how the author acknowledges and responds to conflicting evidence or viewpoints.
Page 107	**CCSS.ELA-Literacy.RI.8.1** Cite the textual evidence that most strongly supports an analysis of what the text says explicitly as well as inferences drawn from the text. **CCSS.ELA-Literacy.RI.8.2** Determine a central idea of a text and analyze its development over the course of the text, including its relationship to supporting ideas; provide an objective summary of the text. **CCSS.ELA-Literacy.RI.8.4** Determine the meaning of words and phrases as they are used in a text, including figurative, connotative, and technical meanings; analyze the impact of specific word choices on meaning and tone, including analogies or allusions to other texts. **CCSS.ELA-Literacy.RI.8.6** Determine an author's point of view or purpose in a text and analyze how the author acknowledges and responds to conflicting evidence or viewpoints.
Pages 108-109	**CCSS.ELA-Literacy.RL.8.1** Cite the textual evidence that most strongly supports an analysis of what the text says explicitly as well as inferences drawn from the text. **CCSS.ELA-Literacy.RL.8.4** Determine the meaning of words and phrases as they are used in a text, including figurative and connotative meanings; analyze the impact of specific word choices on meaning and tone, including analogies or allusions to other texts. **CCSS.ELA-Literacy.L.8.4** Determine or clarify the meaning of unknown and multiple-meaning words or phrases based on grade 8 reading and content, choosing flexibly from a range of strategies.
Page 110	**CCSS.ELA-Literacy.RI.8.1** Cite the textual evidence that most strongly supports an analysis of what the text says explicitly as well as inferences drawn from the text. **CCSS.ELA-Literacy.L.8.4** Determine or clarify the meaning of unknown and multiple-meaning words or phrases based on grade 8 reading and content, choosing flexibly from a range of strategies. **CCSS.ELA-Literacy.W.8.2d** Use precise language and domain-specific vocabulary to inform about or explain the topic.
Pages 111-115	**CCSS.ELA-Literacy.L.8.4c** Consult general and specialized reference materials (e.g., dictionaries, glossaries, thesauruses), both print and digital, to find the pronunciation of a word or determine or clarify its precise meaning or its part of speech.
Page 116	**CCSS.ELA-Literacy.L.8.4c** Consult general and specialized reference materials (e.g., dictionaries, glossaries, thesauruses), both print and digital, to find the pronunciation of a word or determine or clarify its precise meaning or its part of speech. **CCSS.ELA-Literacy.RST.6-8.4** Determine the meaning of symbols, key terms, and other domain-specific words and phrases
Pages 117-118	**CCSS.ELA-Literacy.RI.8.1** Cite the textual evidence that most strongly supports an analysis of what the text says explicitly as well as inferences drawn from the text. **CCSS.ELA-Literacy.W.8.9** Draw evidence from literary or informational texts to support analysis, reflection, and research.
Pages 119-123	**CCSS.ELA-Literacy.RH.6-8.7** Integrate visual information (e.g., in charts, graphs, photographs, videos, or maps) with other information in print and digital texts. **CCSS.ELA-Literacy.RST.6-8.7** Integrate quantitative or technical information expressed in words in a text with a version of that information expressed visually (e.g., in a flowchart, diagram, model, graph, or table). **CCSS.ELA-Literacy.RI.8.1** Cite the textual evidence that most strongly supports an analysis of what the text says explicitly as well as inferences drawn from the text.

Page Number (s)	Common Core State Standards Alignment: Level 8
Pages 124-125	**CCSS.ELA-Literacy.RI.8.1** Cite the textual evidence that most strongly supports an analysis of what the text says explicitly as well as inferences drawn from the text. **CCSS.ELA-Literacy.RI.8.3** Analyze how a text makes connections among and distinctions between individuals, ideas, or events (e.g., through comparisons, analogies, or categories).
Pages 126-130	**CCSS.ELA-Literacy.RL.8.1** Cite the textual evidence that most strongly supports an analysis of what the text says explicitly as well as inferences drawn from the text. **CCSS.ELA-Literacy.RL.8.5** Compare and contrast the structure of two or more texts and analyze how the differing structure of each text contributes to its meaning and style. **CCSS.ELA-Literacy.W.8.9** Draw evidence from literary or informational texts to support analysis, reflection, and research.
Page 131	**CCSS.ELA-Literacy.RI.8.3** Analyze how a text makes connections among and distinctions between individuals, ideas, or events (e.g., through comparisons, analogies, or categories).
Page 132	**CCSS.ELA-Literacy.L.8.1** Demonstrate command of the conventions of standard English grammar and usage when writing or speaking. **CCSS.ELA-Literacy.L.8.2** Demonstrate command of the conventions of standard English capitalization, punctuation, and spelling when writing. **CCSS.ELA-Literacy.L.8.3** Use knowledge of language and its conventions when writing, speaking, reading, or listening.

Understanding prefixes, suffixes, and root words will really help your reading proficiency.

Directions: Use the meanings of the prefixes to help you answer each question with the correct number.

NUMBER, PLEASE...

Prefix	Meaning	Prefix	Meaning
mono-, uni-	one	oct-	eight
du-, di-, bi-	two	dec-	ten
tri-	three	cent-	hundred
quart-, quad-	four	mil-, kilo-	thousand
penta-, cinc-	five	semi-, hemi-	half

1. How many events in a decathlon? _____

2. How many lines in a cinquain poem? _____

3. How many lenses in bifocals? _____

4. How many performers in a trio? _____

5. On what day in May is Cinco de Mayo? _____

6. How many tentacles on an octopus? _____

7. How many singers in a quartet? _____

8. How many sides does the Pentagon building have? _____

9. How many letters in a digraph? _____

10. How many millimeters in a meter? _____

11. How many grams in a kilogram? _____

12. How many rails in a monorail? _____

13. What part of a sphere is a hemisphere? _____

14. How many notes in an octave? _____

15. How many years in a decade? _____

16. If you quadruple something, how many times bigger is it? _____

CHALLENGERS: How often is a bicentennial held? _____

How old is a septuagenarian? _____

Directions: Test your word power. In each description look for the prefix clue. Then write the word being described. Example: opposite of functioning—nonfunctioning.

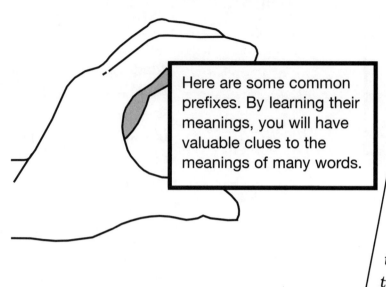

Here are some common prefixes. By learning their meanings, you will have valuable clues to the meanings of many words.

PREFIX	MEANING
anti-	against
bi-	two
centi-	hundred
in-, im-	not
mis-	wrongly
multi-	many
non-	opposite of
pre-	before; ahead of time
re-	again
sub-	under
trans-	change; across
tri-	three

1. opposite of functioning: _____

2. shape with three angles: _____

3. having two poles: _____

4. wrongly understood: _____

5. not patient: _____

6. cycle again: _____

7. against war: _____

8. having many purposes: _____

9. establish before: _____

10. across the Pacific: _____

11. under space: _____

12. change form: _____

13. one-hundredth of a meter: _____

14. opposite of aggressive: _____

15. to submit again: _____

16. not personal: _____

17. of many cultures: _____

18. wrongly interpreted: _____

19. area covering three states: _____

20. determine ahead of time: _____

Directions: In each description look for the suffix clue. Then write the word being described. Example: without fear—fearless.

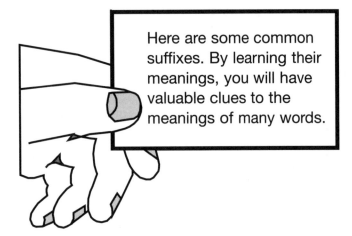

Here are some common suffixes. By learning their meanings, you will have valuable clues to the meanings of many words.

Suffix	Meaning
-able	able to
-en	made of
-ful	filled with
-hood	state of being
-ish	like; approximately
-ity, -ment	state of
-less	without
-let, -ling	small, young
-ly	in a manner
-ness, -ty	having a quality
-ology	the study of
-or, -er, -ist	one who
-ward	in direction of

1. without hope: _____

2. in the state of being a child: _____

3. able to wash: _____

4. one who plays violin: _____

5. in the direction of north: _____

6. like a fool: _____

7. in a state of being content: _____

8. the quality of being kind: _____

9. the quality of being loyal: _____

10. filled with fear: _____

11. one who teaches: _____

12. the study of the mind (psych): _____

13. made of wood: _____

14. a young duck: _____

15. in a strange manner: _____

16. without worth: _____

17. made of gold: _____

18. in a manner of time: _____

19. approximately forty: _____

20. in an up direction: _____

Directions: Venn diagrams are a fun way to classify. When you are done you have a visual picture. Write each word below in the correct space. Note: If the word has no prefix or suffix, write it below the circles.

reappear	appreciate	nonsense	goodness
undone	discover	childish	midnight
poisonous	impossible	wishful	disagreement
dishonesty	adulthood	chemist	recounted
quite	immature	nonworking	frequently
misalign	precooked	uninformed	yellowish

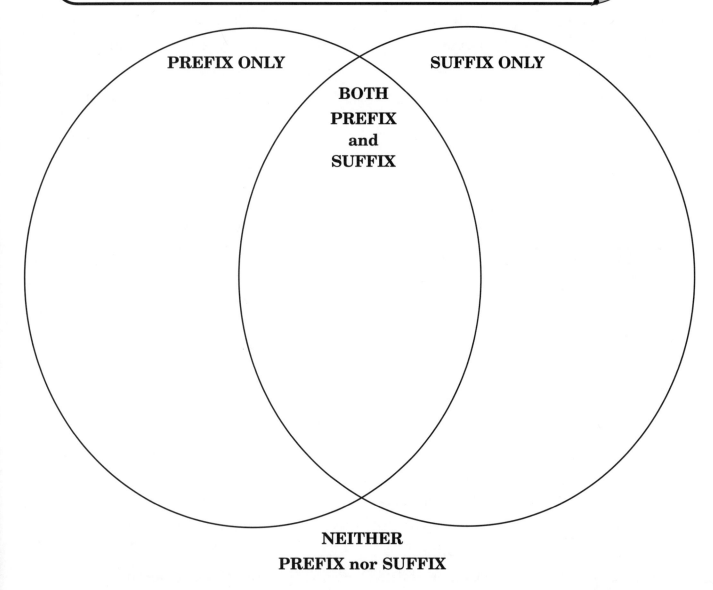

PREFIX ONLY

SUFFIX ONLY

BOTH PREFIX and SUFFIX

NEITHER PREFIX nor SUFFIX

_____

_____

Directions: A large part of our language has its roots in Latin. Study the Latin roots and the English words that were grown from them. Then, match each word to its meaning.

LATIN ROOTS

ROOT	MEANING	EXAMPLE	ROOT	MEANING	EXAMPLE
act	do	enact	ped	foot	pedal
ang	bend	triangle	pop	people	population
aud	hear	audience	rupt	break	erupt
cred	believe	discredit	sign	mark	signal
dict	speak	dictate	spec	see	spectator
fac	make	factory	tract	pull, drag	traction
loc	place	locate	urb	city	urban
man	hand	manual	vac	empty	vacant
mob	move	mobile	vid	see	video

1. incredible   having bends
2. angular   move into action
3. manipulate   one who is on foot
4. audible   speak against
5. relocate   not believable
6. mobilize   move by hand
7. pedestrian   able to be heard
8. contradict   move to a new place
9. abrupt   easy to see
10. suburb   pull toward
11. vivid   liked by people
12. attraction   a sudden break
13. popular   break up or apart
14. disrupt   below or outside the city
15. manufacture   leave a place empty
16. evacuate   seen with the eyes
17. audition   make by hand
18. automobile   the mark of identity
19. evidence   a time to be heard
20. signature   machine that moves by itself

Directions: The roots of our language are widespread. The ones below are Greek. Study them first. Then for each, write two English words (from the list below) that grew from them.

GREEK ROOTS

1. ast: *star*

_____   _____

2. cycl: *circle*

_____   _____

3. graph: *write / draw*

_____   _____

4. gram: *written*

_____   _____

5. meter: *measure*

_____   _____

6. phon: *sound*

_____   _____

7. photo: *light*

_____   _____

8. scop: *see*

_____   _____

9. therm: *heat*

_____   _____

10. bio: *life*

_____   _____

11. geo: *earth*

_____   _____

12. hydr: *water*

_____   _____

13. opt: *eye*

_____   _____

14. phob: *fear*

_____   _____

geography	telephoto
thermos	phonics
periscope	biopsy
asterisk	diagram
phobia	hydrant
cyclone	graphic
diameter	optical
hydroelectric	photosynthesis
autograph	symphony
optometrist	biology
astronomy	claustrophobic
telescope	cyclical
telegram	geology
thermometer (2)	

Directions: Read each word. Pull it apart in your mind. Then write the parts in the correct columns. The first one is done for you.

	PREFIX	ROOT WORD	SUFFIX
1. hostess		host	ess
2. discomfort			
3. redefine			
4. import			
5. annually			
6. uncertainty			
7. thoughtless			
8. mispronounce			
9. government			
10. joyous			
11. irregular			
12. antisocial			
13. misleading			
14. uncomfortable			
15. sorrowful			
16. knighthood			
17. subcategory			

You're on a roll! Now find three words in one of your textbooks: one with a root word plus a prefix, one with a root word plus a suffix, and one with both. Write them below.

18. _____			
19. _____			
20. _____			

© Saddleback Educational Publishing • www.sdlback.com
Common Core Skills & Strategies for Reading: Level 8

Refresh your skills with recognizing plurals and possessives.

Directions: Test your ability to tell the difference between a plural and a possessive. Remember: a plural means more than one; a possessive shows ownership. Fill in the bubble that describes the word in bold. Remember: some words are both plural *and* possessive.

1. **Maria's** cat seems to sleep all day.	O plural	O possessive
2. The **boys'** gloves lay by the bench.	O plural	O possessive
3. Thunderous **clouds** loomed in the distance.	O plural	O possessive
4. The **girl's** makeup was too heavy.	O plural	O possessive
5. The bird preened **its** feathers.	O plural	O possessive
6. Loud **noises** came from the barn.	O plural	O possessive
7. **Dr. Raymond's** office was crowded.	O plural	O possessive
8. The **planks** creaked as we walked across.	O plural	O possessive
9. A big ship can withstand pounding **waves**.	O plural	O possessive
10. I'm always finding Rex's **toys** in my room.	O plural	O possessive
11. The **flowers'** petals were soft and delicate.	O plural	O possessive
12. I hardly recognized the **Browns'** children.	O plural	O possessive
13. An **artist's** style is unique.	O plural	O possessive
14. The **trees'** branches were laden with snow.	O plural	O possessive
15. The moon's gravity causes **Earth's** tides.	O plural	O possessive
16. **Whales** migrate thousands of miles.	O plural	O possessive
17. Caroline thought your **brother's** car was cool.	O plural	O possessive
18. The **beaches** are patrolled day and night.	O plural	O possessive
19. Dad went to **Uncle Jeff's** to go fishing.	O plural	O possessive
20. In the cave hung **hundreds** of bats.	O plural	O possessive

Reading is like detective work. Clues to unknown words can be found right among the words around it. This strategy is called using context clues, and it works!

Directions: Use context clues to figure out the meaning of the bold word. Write it on the line.

1. In math class, Jen passed the note to Sara **discreetly**.

_____

2. The thirsty man **yearned** for a drink of water.

_____

3. The miner struck a new **lode** of coal.

_____

4. Old age did not **hamper** him one bit.

_____

5. The explorers were running short on **provisions**.

_____

6. Pirates were caught red-handed with the **contraband**.

_____

7. Without shots, the animals were **susceptible** to disease.

_____

8. This is only a **facsimile**—the real gem is in the safe.

_____

9. The tiny infant remained in the **neonatal** ward.

_____

10. The tornado threatened to **annihilate** the small town.

_____

11. Unlike other **felines**, lions live in groups.

_____

12. Dad said nothing, but just nodded **affirmatively**.

_____

- necessities
- strongly wished for
- hold back; adversely affect
- in a positive way
- destroy
- newborn
- vulnerable to attack
- look alike; copy
- in a secretive way
- stolen goods
- members of the cat family
- vein of mineral ore

NAME _____   DATE _____

Directions: Read the story. Use context clues to figure out the possible meanings of the words in bold. Then write them next to their meanings below.

Family Fun

Last month we took a trip to Southern California for my cousin's wedding. By the **scowl** on my face when Mom told us we were going, she knew I was less than thrilled. So the next **declaration** out of her mouth was that, besides going to the wedding (**drudge**, drudge), we would also be going to the Zoo Safari Park AND the water park. Okay! I decided I could sit through the wedding and even be **hospitable** for a few hours.

During the ceremony I was **catatonic**, but the reception wasn't too bad. There were **copious** amounts of food and their choice of music was **palatable**. It was over in a flash and the next day we were on to better things.

The Zoo Safari Park was awesome. No cages or enclosures—just open **range** for giraffes, zebras, and other creatures to roam. The **docent** said as long as we adhered to the rules, everyone (us and the animals) would be safe.

The next day we **donned** our swimsuits for a day at the water park. Mom was a **trifle** tired, so she just **reclined** under a shady tree and read a book. The rest of us did the slides, the tubes, the wave machine—stopped for a snack—then did it all again.

That night I wrote a thank-you note to my cousin Irene for the great time we had (at her wedding, of course).

1. hard, tedious work: _____

2. tour guide: _____

3. abundant; plentiful: _____

4. a small amount; a bit: _____

5. leaned or lay back to rest: _____

6. put on or dressed in: _____

7. open area of land for grazing: _____

8. statement; announcement: _____

9. a frowning facial expression: _____

10. friendly, sociable toward guests: _____

11. pleasant or acceptable to the taste or mind: _____

12. unmoving; seemingly without thought or action: _____

NAME _____   DATE _____

Directions: Here are two chances to show your context clue power. Just follow the directions.

A. When Noreen wanted the space adjacent to her sister Karen's room for her computer, Karen got agitated. An argument ensued. Dad had to be called in to adjudicate the dispute. Karen finally acquiesced to Noreen's plan.

Find the word in the story that best matches each meaning:

1. consented without protest: _____

2. act as judge: _____

3. annoyed: _____

4. followed immediately: _____

5. next to; beside: _____

Describe a time you acquiesced to someone: _____

_____

_____

_____

B. Sam is an amateur ichthyologist—he has several tanks of fresh and saltwater fish in his room. He has plenty of equipment to ensure his fish are happy and healthy— air pumps to infuse the water with bubbles so that it is properly aerated, filters to remove contaminates, and heaters to prevent hypothermia.

Find the word in the story that best matches each meaning:

1. put in; inject: _____

2. person who studies fish: _____

3. below normal temperature: _____

4. supply with oxygen: _____

5. impurities: _____

Complete this statement: I consider myself an amateur _____.

Now describe your activities related to this subject, interest, or hobby: _____

_____

_____

_____

Directions: Complete the puzzle by using a simpler word for the one in bold. You can look in the help box (below right), but be careful—there are words you won't use included.

ACROSS

1. The boat began to **keel** over.
3. Grandpa cannot **recollect** how he got that scar.
5. The king lifted his **chalice** to toast the knights.
6. After working on his truck, Joe was covered in **grime**.
8. She **loathed** having to clean the horses' stalls.
10. These **faux** pearls look like the real thing!
11. The speaker's joke evoked a big **guffaw**.

DOWN

1. The soldier stuck by his **comrade**.
2. Night came and the children fell into a deep **slumber**.
4. The officers **hoisted** the flag.
5. You seem to have no **option** but to go.
7. We watched it **metamorphose** right before our eyes.
9. They began to **converse** in Spanish.

dirt	grease
fall	sink
army	friend
remember	collect
boards	sleep
urn	cup
talk	write
folded	raised
loved	hated
change	die
white	fake
way	choice
laugh	sigh

Directions: Use what you know about context clues to navigate this story. Fill in the missing words.

Who Discovered America?

Paragraph 1:

mutiny

disgruntled

technically

True, in 1492 Columbus sailed the ocean blue, and just as his crews became so _____ that they threatened _____ so they could return to Spain, land was spotted. This was an island in the Bahamas. Though _____ this was only a part of "America" Columbus never set foot on the mainland.

Paragraph 2:

prior

preceded

bolster

notoriety

arrived

Despite Columbus' _____, plenty of archaeological evidence exists to _____ the claim that a number of others _____ him. Norseman Leif Erikson not only reached North America, he established a colony in Newfoundland 500 years _____ to Columbus. But even this Viking was not the first. Another Norseman, Bjarni Herjolfsson _____ in 985 or 986.

Paragraph 3:

construed

continents

context

popular

By definition, the Americas include the _____ of North and South America, but _____ use of the term "America" is _____ to mean the United States. In this _____, the first European to discover America would be Spanish explorer Ponce de Leon, who "found" and named Florida in 1513.

Paragraph 4:

previously

thriving

perspective

Obviously

These and other adventurers were among the first of their cultures to "discover" America. From their _____, they had indeed uncovered something _____ unknown. _____, there were already many people and cultures _____ in North America when they arrived. Can one "discover" what already exists? It depends on your point of view.

Give your point of view about the question posed at the end of the passage: _____

_____

_____

_____

Directions: Read each text excerpt. Use context clues to help you complete the statements.

A. A botanical garden is an area of flora in which plants are grown chiefly for scientific, educational, or aesthetic purposes. They usually surround an institution, such as a university or museum.

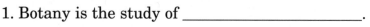

1. Botany is the study of _____.

2. A synonym for plants is _____.

3. A word that means pleasing to the senses is _____.

4. A university may have botanical gardens for the purpose of _____.

5. True or false: All botanical gardens are open to the public. _____

B. Beech is the name of a family of trees that grows in the temperate regions of North America and Europe. It has papery leaves and slender twigs. Its fruit, beechnuts, are edible. Its wood is used for making furniture and for fuel.

1. Beechnuts are the _____ of the beech tree.

2. A synonym for areas is _____.

3. The word _____ describes a seasonal climate.

4. A word that means able to be eaten is _____.

5. True or false: Beech trees have paper leaves. _____

C. The era covering the presidency of James Polk was known as the "Fabulous Forties." During this time the American flag was raised over much of the western territory, Texas became a member of the Union, gold was discovered in California, covered wagons rolled over the Oregon trail, and Americans sang Stephen Foster's "Oh, Susanna."

1. The Union refers to the _____.

2. A word meaning period of time is _____.

3. Is "Oh, Susanna" a story, a song, or a campaign slogan? _____

4. What state entered the Union during Polk's presidency? _____

5. True or false: Polk was president during the 1940s. _____

Directions: Use context clues to figure out what the bold word means. Fill in the correct bubble.

1. Having the forms filled out ahead of time will **expedite** the process.

   O explain in detail

   O speed up; make easier

   O neither

2. The teacher was suspicious when she noticed the **parity** of the two friends' reports.

   O similarity; resemblance

   O spelling errors

   O neither

3. The warrior carried a shield and **saber**.

   O gun

   O cannon

   O neither

4. After the horse show, Donna carefully put all the horse's **tack** away.

   O hay and feed

   O riding equipment

   O neither

5. When Josh's pet rabbit died, his friend Dave was unable to **console** him.

   O reach by phone

   O comfort; cheer up

   O neither

6. Good news is cause for **jubilation**.

   O concern

   O joy and celebration

   O neither

7. The rain forest was **lush** with flowers, birds, and insects.

   O heavily filled

   O wet

   O neither

8. When Cynthia connected on a map her city with New York and Chicago, they formed an **isosceles** triangle.

   O cold; frigid

   O having two equal-length sides

   O neither

9. The mules were **laden** with packs.

   O laying down

   O scoop for liquids

   O neither

10. The story of the sinking of the Titanic will be presented in three **episodes**.

    O parts in a series

    O events or occurrences

    O neither

11. Nothing could **compel** Kris to believe the stories about UFOs.

    O turn away from

    O convince; persuade

    O neither

12. The man only confessed under **duress**.

    O threat of force

    O bright lights

    O neither

NAME _____   DATE _____

Directions: Read the story and the statements. Decide if each statement is true, false, or can't be determined from the information given in the story. Write TRUE, FALSE, or UNKNOWN.

The Pangolin

In parts of southeastern Asia, Indonesia, and areas of Africa below the Sahara desert, lives a relic of prehistory. The pangolin is a creature that looks something like a cross between an anteater and an armadillo. It is classified in the spiny anteater family, but instead of the coarse hair found on Central or South American anteaters, the pangolin have coats of mail formed by overlapping scales. Like their Central or South American cousins, pangolins have long tails, long, narrow snouts, and a sticky flypaper-like tongues, which they can thrust out to catch their meals.

Pangolins have an effective means of defense. In addition to being protected by their scales, they also can roll up into a tight ball. Most enemies are deterred, but people in some areas of their range consider pangolin meat a delicacy.

_____ 1. No pangolins live in North America.

_____ 2. Pigs and pangolins have similar snouts.

_____ 3. Pangolins eat ants.

_____ 4. Some people eat pangolins.

_____ 5. Pangolins can be 3–5 feet long.

_____ 6. The Sahara desert is in Africa.

_____ 7. Pangolins have coarse hair.

_____ 8. Armadillos have coarse hair.

_____ 9. The pangolin is a type of armadillo.

_____ 10. Deterred means encouraged.

_____ 11. One meaning of mail is flexible armor.

_____ 12. Central or South American anteaters have soft, pliable hair.

_____ 13. A relic is something preserved from the past.

_____ 14. American anteaters have sticky tongues.

_____ 15. In this story's context, delicacy means fragile beauty.

_____ 16. Pangolins are shy and hunt at night.

_____ 17. A pangolin's preferred food is flies.

_____ 18. Pangolins can tuck in their limbs to form a sphere.

_____ 19. In this story's context, thrust means to fling forward.

_____ 20. Pangolins have large, strong claws.

© Saddleback Educational Publishing • www.sdlback.com

Directions: Clues in statements below will help you figure out what mystery thing he or she is describing. First pick out five words in the statements that you are not totally familiar with. Use a dictionary to define them on the note squares. Next, match the person's name to the correct object. Then complete the statements with the identifying word. One is done for you.

Don "It is an instrument that indicates time by the position of a shadow cast by the sun on a flat surface. It is a ___sundial___."

Lisa "It is an immense and extremely luminous star with a diameter at least 100X that of the sun. It is a _____."

Tanya "It is an instrument used by navigators for measuring angular distance between the sun or other star and the horizon. It is a _____."

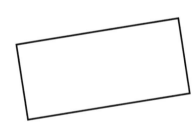

Deion "It is the contractile circular dark opening in the center of the iris of the eye. It is a _____."

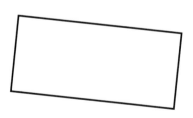

Chris "It is the meteor shower visible annually in November that appears to radiate from the constellation Leo. It is the _____."

Pedro "It is any giving off of light caused by absorption of radiant energy that is perceived as a glow. It is _____."

_____ 1. supergiant   _____ 4. pupil

_____ 2. luminescence   _____ 5. Leonids

_____ 3. sextant   ___Don___ 6. sundial

NAME _____   DATE _____

Directions: Have you ever tried explaining something to a little kid? You use basic words and simple concepts. Try doing that here by rephrasing each statement so a young child could understand it.

1. A colony of hornets had migrated into the gables of the house.

   _____

   _____

   _____

   _____

2. The two kings called a truce to end the hostilities between their kingdoms.

   _____

   _____

   _____

3. Every time Jimmy had to do something tedious, he procrastinated.

   _____

   _____

   _____

   _____

4. The perfume contained several elements, including a derivative of the jasmine plant.

   _____

   _____

   _____

   _____

Directions: Using the clues in the sentences, write what you think the bold word means. Next, check your answers against the definitions in a dictionary. Finally, evaluate your predictions.

1. When we finally moved from an apartment to a house, the rooms seemed palatial.

   I think **palatial** means_____.

   The dictionary says it means _____.

   I was (check one) ☐ right on   ☐ close   ☐ way off

2. There seems to be a glut of toys on the market tied to popular movies.

   I think **glut** means_____.

   The dictionary says it means _____.

   I was (check one) ☐ right on   ☐ close   ☐ way off

3. The bride wore a taffeta gown and a gossamer veil.

   I think **gossamer** means_____.

   The dictionary says it means_____.

   I was (check one) ☐ right on   ☐ close   ☐ way off

4. The old man's face looked like a vulture's; his fingers like talons.

   I think **talon** means_____.

   The dictionary says it means _____.

   I was (check one) ☐ right on   ☐ close   ☐ way off

5. She lectured for an hour before reaching the pivotal information.

   I think **pivotal** means_____.

   The dictionary says it means _____.

   I was (check one) ☐ right on   ☐ close   ☐ way off

Discovering how things are related is an important reading skill, and an analogy is a type of comparison. The trick to understanding analogies is in figuring out how the words are related.

Directions: Read each analogy below. Think about what is being compared. Then match it to the correct relationship. The first one is done for you.

1. *baby* is to *babies* as *mouse* is to *mice*   PART to WHOLE

2. *car* is to *seats* as *desk* is to *drawers*   WHOLE to PART

3. *wick* is to *candle* as *string* is to *yo-yo*   SINGULAR to PLURAL

4. *wrote* is to *write* as *sang* is to *sing*   PLURAL to SINGULAR

5. *children* is to *child* as *ladies* is to *lady*   PAST to PRESENT

6. *lemon* is to *sour* as *cake* is to *sweet*   PRESENT to PAST

7. *giving* is to *gave* as *seeing* is to *saw*   CHARACTERISTICS

8. *flying* is to *bird* as *swimming* is to *fish*   LOCATION

9. *whale* is to *ocean* as *deer* is to *woods*   OBJECT to ACTION

10. *nose* is to *smell* as *eyes* are to *see*   ACTION to OBJECT

11. *second* is to *first* as *Tuesday* is to *Monday*   CLASSIFICATION

12. *moth* is to *insect* as *snake* is to *reptile*   COUNTERPART

13. *huge* is to *large* as *begin* is to *start*   SEQUENCE

14. *quiet* is to *loud* as *hard* is to *soft*   SYNONYMS (same)

15. *cow* is to *calf* as *cat* is to *kitten*   ANTONYMS (opposite)

CHALLENGER! Here are more analogies. This time see if you can complete the second part.

16. *hoot* is to *owl* as *lion* is to _____

17. *woman* is to *aunt* as *man* is to _____

18. *is* is to *was* as *go* is to _____

19. *you are* is to *you're* as *we are* is to _____

20. *less* is to *least* as *more* is to _____

21. *in* is to *entrance* as *out* is to _____

NAME _____   DATE _____

Directions: You are to analogies as a star is to movies! Prove it now.

A. *These analogies compare part to whole or whole to part. Fill in the missing word.*

1. *oar* is to <u>*boat*</u> as *propeller* is to _____

2. *pie* is to <u>*crust*</u> as *cake* is to _____

3. *tree* is to <u>*sap*</u> as *person* is to _____

4. *lid* is to <u>*jar*</u> as *cap* is to _____

5. *violin* is to <u>*strings*</u> as *piano* is to _____

6. *stinger* is to <u>*bee*</u> as *fangs* are to _____

7. *porcupine* is to <u>*quills*</u> as *cat* is to _____

8. *peel* is to <u>*banana*</u> as *husk* is to _____

9. *flipper* is to <u>*seal*</u> as *hoof* is to _____

10. *stem* is to <u>*plant*</u> as *trunk* is to _____

B. *These analogies compare action to object or object to action. Fill in the missing word.*

1. *lizard* is to <u>*crawl*</u> as *rabbit* is to _____

2. *honk* is to <u>*horn*</u> as *ring* is to _____

3. *wink* is to <u>*eye*</u> as *sniff* is to _____

4. *pencil* is to <u>*draw*</u> as *brush* is to _____

5. *knife* is to <u>*cut*</u> as *drum* is to _____

6. *sponge* is to <u>*scrub*</u> as *broom* is to _____

7. *author* is to <u>*write*</u> as *illustrator* is to _____

8. *ski* is to <u>*snow*</u> as *swim* is to _____

9. *shovel* is to <u>*dig*</u> as *hammer* is to _____

10. *zip* is to <u>*jacket*</u> as *lock* is to _____

NAME _____ DATE _____

Directions: These analogies compare the characteristics or properties listed on the notes on the left. Complete each analogy. Then write on each note the numbers of the analogies that apply to that characteristic or property. The first one is done for you.

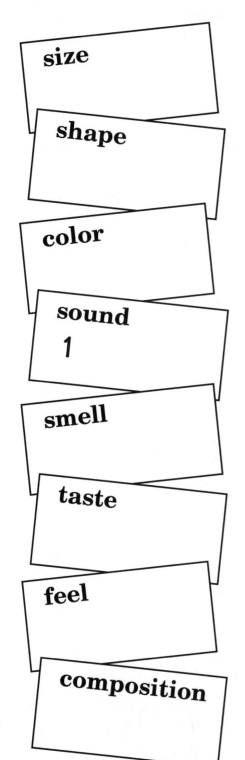

size

shape

color

sound
1

smell

taste

feel

composition

1. *purr* is to *soft* as *thunder* is to __loud__

2. *sweet* is to *candy* as *sour* is to _____

3. *box* is to *square* as *ball* is to _____

4. *fence* is to *wood* as *window* is to _____

5. *hippo* is to *gigantic* as *ant* is to _____

6. *blue* is to *sky* as *green* is to _____

7. *fragrant* is to *flower* as *stink* is to _____

8. *rock* is to *hard* as *pillow* is to _____

9. *apple* is to *red* as *banana* is to _____

10. *cloth* is to *shirt* as *rubber* is to _____

11. *smooth* is to *silk* as *rough* is to _____

12. *moon* is to *sphere* as *pyramid* is to _____

13. *paper* is to *book* as *wool* is to _____

14. *cluck* is to *chicken* as *neigh* is to _____

15. *tart* is to *grapefruit* as *salty* is to _____

16. *tree* is to *tall* as *bush* is to _____

17. *tangy* is to *lemonade* as *sweet* is to _____

18. *plains* are to *flat* as *mountains* are to _____

19. *antiseptic* is to *hospital* as *musty* is to _____

20. *screech* is to *owl* as *hiss* is to _____

Directions: An analogy contains two pairs of words. Each pair is related in the same way. It is easiest to complete an analogy when the last word is missing. On this page, you will have to figure out the missing word in any position.

These analogies compare object to action or action to object. Fill in the missing word.

1. _fly_ is to _plane_ as _____ is to _car_

2. _ruler_ is to _measure_ as _book_ is to _____

3. _____ is to _water_ as _eat_ is to _food_

4. _blink_ is to _____ as _swallow_ is to _mouth_

5. _write_ is to _pen_ as _____ is to _keyboard_

6. _bed_ is to _sleep_ as _bathtub_ is to _____

7. _____ is to _nose_ as _taste_ is to _tongue_

8. _bark_ is to _____ as _meow_ is to _cat_

9. _____ is to _boil_ as _pan_ is to _bake_

10. _gallop_ is to _horse_ as _____ is to _frog_

11. _doctor_ is to _people_ as _vet_ is to _____

12. _television_ is to _____ as _radio_ is to _listen_

13. _____ are to _breathe_ as _stomach_ is to _digest_

14. _drum_ is to _beat_ as _whistle_ is to _____

15. _hose_ is to _water_ as _____ is to _dig_

16. _____ is to _chill_ as _oven_ is to _heat_

17. _swim_ is to _shark_ as _____ is to _eagle_

18. _____ is to _knife_ as _bond_ is to _glue_

19. _preen_ is to _____ as _brush_ is to _hair_

20. _carpenter_ is to _build_ as _mechanic_ is to _____

Directions: There are four kinds of analogies on this page. Each fits into one of the categories based on how the words are related. For each analogy, first write the letter of the category that best applies to it. Then, complete it with an appropriate word.

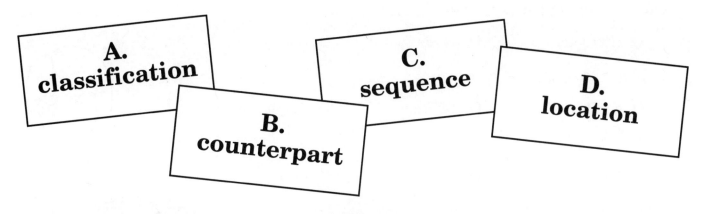

A. classification

B. counterpart

C. sequence

D. location

EXAMPLES:

_____**A**_____ *Saturn* is to *planet* as *Atlantic* is to *ocean*
_____**B**_____ *waiter* is to *waitress* as *actor* is to *actress*
_____**C**_____ *spring* is to *summer* as *Friday* is to *Saturday*
_____**D**_____ *stove* is to *kitchen* as *clothes* are to *closet*

_____ 1. *beginning* is to *end* as *start* is to _____

_____ 2. *joey* is to *kangaroo* as *cub* is to _____

_____ 3. *roof* is to *house* as *hat* is to _____

_____ 4. *soccer* is to *sport* as *apple* is to _____

_____ 5. *tadpole* is to *frog* as *caterpillar* is to _____

_____ 6. *uncle* is to *nephew* as *aunt* is to _____

_____ 7. *breakfast* is to *lunch* as *lunch* is to _____

_____ 8. *judge* is to *courtroom* as *teacher* is to _____

_____ 9. *tree* is to *redwood* as *toy* is to _____

_____ 10. *forty* is to *thirty* as *sixty* is to _____

_____ 11. *bracelet* is to *wrist* as *ring* is to _____

_____ 12. *chair* is to *furniture* as *robin* is to _____

Directions: These analogies are synonyms (same meaning) or antonyms (opposite meaning). Determine which is which, then fill in the bubble of the word that correctly completes the analogy.

1. *labor* is to *work* as *story* is to _____

     O character   O words   O tale

2. *often* is to *seldom* as *same* is to _____

     O similar   O different   O frequently

3. *aid* is to *help* as *depart* is to _____

     O leave   O schedule   O finish

4. *found* is to *lost* as *create* is to _____

     O make   O find   O destroy

5. *sob* is to *cry* as *giggle* is to _____

     O funny   O laugh   O joke

6. *seize* is to *grab* as *attempt* is to _____

     O convince   O try   O hold

7. *cruel* is to *kind* as *together* is to _____

     O apart   O friends   O joined

8. *response* is to *answer* as *walk* is to _____

     O reply   O stroll   O run

9. *different* is to *varied* as *required* is to_____

     O unnecessary   O unique   O needed

10. *never* is to *always* as *none* is to _____

     O nothing   O all   O few

11. *noise* is to *silence* as *follow* is to _____

     O leader   O directions   O lead

12. *single* is to *one* as *difficult* is to _____

     O hard   O unit   O easy

Note this note: Park by the park. A good reader has to be on the lookout for words with more than one meaning.

Directions: Many words have multiple meanings. If the meaning you know doesn't work in a sentence, look the word up in a dictionary. Others you know all the meanings of and it's just a matter of figuring out which applies. Below are multiple meanings for three familiar words. Write the number of the meaning that applies in the sentence given.

_____ A.   Mom left me a note about practice.

_____ B.   I can't sing a note.

_____ C.   Edison was an inventor of note.

_____ D.   Note the differences between the two insects.

note:
1. short written message
2. to call or pay attention to   3. distinction, quality, or importance   4. a musical sound

_____ E.   Dad works at the industrial park.

_____ F.   Do not park by the red curb.

_____ G.   We played baseball at the park.

_____ H.   We went to the amusement park.

park:
1. to stop a vehicle in a space   2. an open area for public recreation
3. an area set aside for a commercial use

_____ I.   Did you wear your watch today?

_____ J.   Watch me do a high dive.

_____ K.   Watch for rattlesnakes in this area.

_____ L.   Will you watch my dog while I'm away?

_____ M.   Security is on watch at the bank.

_____ N.   The night watch ends at 6:00 a.m.

watch:
1. guard   2. to take care of   3. to be on the lookout   4. to observe casually   5. a timepiece carried or worn   6. the period of time a guard is on duty

Directions: When you encounter a word with multiple meanings you have to figure out its usage. Below is an example. Use the given definitions to help you figure out how the word is used in each sentence. Write the meaning. Then write a sentence of your own using the word with that meaning.

MINT *noun*
1. **a place where money is coined by authority of the government**
2. **a huge or unlimited amount or supply**
3. **new or in its original form**
4. **any of various plants used for flavoring and aroma**
5. **candy flavored with extract of a plant in that family**

A) After dinner, the waiter brought us each a **mint**.

meaning: _____

your sentence: _____

_____

B) He bought the collectible model in **mint** condition.

meaning: _____

your sentence: _____

_____

C) The group had a **mint** of ideas about redesigning the playground area.

meaning: _____

your sentence: _____

_____

D) While visiting the capital, we toured the U.S. **Mint**.

meaning: _____

your sentence: _____

_____

E) Place some **mint** leaves in areas you want your cat to avoid.

meaning: _____

your sentence: _____

_____

NAME _____ DATE _____

Directions: The bold word has multiple meanings. Write what you think it means in each sentence. Next check the various meanings in a dictionary. Write the meaning that best applies. Then evaluate your prediction.

1. She felt that being grounded for a week was just punishment for her actions.

   In this sentence I think **just** means_____.

   The dictionary meaning that applies is _____.

   I was (check one) ☐ right on   ☐ close   ☐ way off

2. The tourists had to pay a duty on items bought while they were in Europe.

   I think **duty** means _____.

   The dictionary meaning that applies is _____.

   I was (check one) ☐ right on   ☐ close   ☐ way off

3. Even the boom of thunder did not rouse him from slumber.

   I think **rouse** means _____.

   The dictionary meaning that applies is _____.

   I was (check one) ☐ right on   ☐ close   ☐ way off

4. When flying to the Orient, even the seats in coach are expensive.

   I think **coach** means _____.

   The dictionary meaning that applies is _____.

   I was (check one) ☐ right on   ☐ close   ☐ way off

5. From a very early age, Leah had a fancy for horses.

   I think **fancy** means_____.

   The dictionary meaning that applies is _____.

   I was (check one) ☐ right on   ☐ close   ☐ way off

Directions: As you read, always ask yourself if what you just read makes sense. If it doesn't, it could mean there is a word with multiple meanings. Try other meanings for the word, then reread. If you are still stumped, check the dictionary. Try this strategy with the story below.

A Rough Morning

It was the first day of school and Josh knew it wasn't going to be a good one. It was only 8:10 and he was already running late and had already gotten into a row with his mother. As he tore down the path to catch the bus, he felt bad about leaving his mom still sore. After all, she was right—he should have gotten up when the alarm went off. The driver waited just a moment before shutting the bus doors.

Josh froze in his tracks as he watched the bus pull away. Now he would have to go back home and not only face his mom, but also ask her for a ride to school. Josh squeezed his eyes tight for a moment, then opened them wide. (His mom said this relieves tension. He hoped she was doing it, too.) Then he shoved his hands into his pockets and walked back home.

Mom didn't even look shocked to see him when he came back in the door. It was more of a glare. Josh knew what that meant—I told you so. Rather than trump up some defense for himself, he just apologized and sweetly asked for a ride to school. Mom's face softened and she went to get her keys.

Underline the correct meaning of each word below as it is used in this story:

1. **running**:	in a condition of	moving swiftly by foot
2. **row**:	use oars to propel	quarrel or squabble
3. **tore**:	rip into pieces	moved very quickly
4. **catch**:	overtake; get to	grab or snare
5. **froze**:	turned into ice	stopped motionless
6. **face**:	confront	part of the head
7. **tension**:	amount of stretch	mental stress
8. **glare**:	bright light	disapproving look
9. **trump**:	create; invent	an advantage
10. **softened**:	became gentler	became less loud

Answer these questions.

11. In paragraph 1, does **row** rhyme with *tow* or *cow*? _____

12. What was Mom sore about? _____

13. Why wasn't Mom shocked to see Josh back home? _____

_____

14. What made Mom get over being mad? _____

15. Did Josh believe he was right or wrong? _____

Directions: Some words mean one thing as a noun (naming word) and another thing as a verb (action word). For each sentence, write N or V under the bold word. Then write the correct meaning of each word. The first one is done for you.

     (1)   (2)

A. The **bat** began to **bat** its wings.
     n   v

(1) __flying mammal__   (2) ____flutter____

v. flutter

n. flying mammal

            (3)

B. The three billy goats began to climb the **bluff** knowing they

        (4)

   had been able to **bluff** the troll.

(3) _____   (4) _____

n. steep cliff

v. mislead; fool

     (5)   (6)

C. The **slip** of paper should **slip** into the envelope.

(5) _____   (6) _____

v. move easily

n. thin piece

       (7)   (8)

D. The stripes on the **hide** of a tiger helps it **hide** among
   the grasses.

(7) _____   (8) _____

v. conceal

n. animal skin

       (9)

D. The man began to **tire** in the desert heat while changing

      (10)

   the flat **tire**.

n. rubber wheel

v. grow weary

(9) _____   (10) _____

Being able to recognize and use synonyms and antonyms gives your reading and writing power a boost.

Directions: Synonyms are words that mean the same or almost the same. For example, great, wonderful, terrific, and super have similar meanings; they are synonyms. Pick out the synonyms in a list and a story (below).

A. *Circle any words that are synonyms for the bold word. Use a dictionary if needed.*

1. **catch**	grab	fly	seize	nab	squeeze	entrap
2. **affix**	bond	confirm	attach	repair	fasten
3. **spread**	position	spew	scatter	disperse	diffuse
4. **calm**	placid	ruffled	serene	tranquil	still
5. **invent**	devise	concoct	formulate	infer	clever
6. **ask**	request	inquire	aspire	answer	question
7. **labor**	manual	toil	work	earn	contract	lend
8. **infrequent**	sporadic	scarce	often	profuse	rare

B. *Read the passage. Match each bold word to a synonym in the story. Write it on the line.*

With its **victim** in **view**—**typically** a young, old, **ill**, or stray animal—a cheetah will casually **stalk** toward it. When within a **range** of about 100 yards, it will begin to **sprint**. The herd will **disperse** and the cheetah will **swiftly** overtake the intended kill. Because of the cheetah's great speed, the chase is usually over in **mere** seconds.

1. sick _____

2. quickly _____

3. sight _____

4. stride _____

5. usually _____

6. prey _____

7. distance _____

8. run _____

9. scatter _____

10. only _____

Directions: Antonymns are words that mean the opposite from one another. Happy and sad, fast and slow, light and dark are all antonymns. Find the antonyms in the activities below.

A. *For each bold word below, circle its antonym in the list that follows.*

1. **told**	answered	asked	replied	questioned	
2. **least**	less	more	most	fewest	fewer
3. **remain**	stay	concur	steadfast	change	
4. **lose**	tight	find	lost	lend	firm
5. **prohibit**	stop	avoid	defend	allow	deter
6. **create**	destroy	invent	cover	build	decay
7. **sure**	positive	wishful	uncertain	negative	
8. **nothing**	often	none	something	zero	several

B. *Replace the bold word in each sentence with an antonym. Spell it out in the blanks. The letters given will remind you what antonyms are and give you a clue to each answer.*

1. Most athletes are healthy and **weak**. 	 __ __ __ **o** __ __

2. The ocean is **shallow**. 	 __ __ __ **p**

3. My stomach was **full** and growling for food. 	 __ __ **p** __ __

4. I saw the unhappy **smile** on her face. 	 __ __ **o** __ __

5. It was hot and the temperature began to **fall**. 	 __ __ **s** __

6. This sweater may **grow** in the dryer. 	 __ __ __ **i** __ __

7. I will never **remember** you. 	 __ __ __ __ __ **t**

8. Mice chewed a **narrow** hole in the wall. 	 __ __ __ **e**

9. Mrs. Kaplan said we're being too **quiet**. 	 __ __ __ **s** __ __

Directions: The clues below ask you to supply a synonym or antonym for a word. You can look in the box for help, but be careful—there are extra words you won't use.

ACROSS

1. antonym for slow
3. synonym for wonderful
5. antonym for adore
7. synonym for job
9. antonym for bright
10. synonym for imitate
11. antonym for worthless
12. synonym for freedom
13. synonym for truthful

DOWN

1. antonym for plentiful
2. antonym for genuine
3. antonym for minimum
4. antonym for dull
5. synonym for vanish
6. antonym for ignite
8. synonym for obstinate

valuable	scarce
awful	disappear
tusk	finish
fake	real
sharp	task
swift	dim
love	boring
least	extinguish
despise	useless
honest	copy
laborious	maximum
shiny	confinement
stubborn	friendly
liberty	marvelous
light	frightened

Directions: Read the passage, then find the requested synonyms and antonyms in the text. Write your answers on the lines. Consult a dictionary if necessary.

Mercury's Different Forms

When you hear the word Mercury, what do you envision—the planet, a silvery liquid metal, or the ancient **messenger** of the Roman gods? Actually, the planet and the metal are named after the Roman god.

Compared with the knowledge we have **amassed** today, the Romans knew little astronomy. But they were **keen** observers of the **heavens** and were **cognizant** of the look and movements of objects in the sky. They believed that the faster an object moved across the sky, the nearer to Earth it must be. The planet Mercury moves more **rapidly** than the other planets, so it was named after the speedy messenger of the Roman gods, **frequently** depicted with wings on his helmet and sandals. We know, of course, that Mercury moves faster, not because it is closer to Earth, but because it is closer to the sun.

But what did this **ancient** Roman god have to do with the liquid metal that you may see in thermometers? The metal mercury is also known as quicksilver. The "silver" in this alias is **obvious**. The "quick" actually has two meanings: "live" and "fast". Quicksilver at room temperature forms shiny liquid drops and moves with such **ease** that it seems to be alive.

1. synonym for accumulated:

_____

2. antonym for modern:

_____

3. synonym for sharp:

_____

4. synonym for skies:

_____

5. antonym for slowly:

_____

6. antonym for difficulty:

_____

7. antonym for seldom:

_____

8. synonym for dispatcher:

_____

9. antonym for unaware:

_____

10. antonym for concealed:

_____

CHALLENGER: What term means the same as "another name for"? _____

Homonyms are words that sound alike but have different meanings and spellings.

Directions: Most homonyms are easy to read, but if you let them slip by unidentified, they can throw off your comprehension. Select the correct homonym for the questions below.

1. Would a story be read **aloud** or **allowed**? _____

2. Would you be **build** or **billed** for a purchase? _____

3. Would you make bread with **dough** or **doe**? _____

4. Would a house have a **cellar** or **seller**? _____

5. Would an animal have **fir** or **fur**? _____

6. Would you wash your **close** or **clothes**? _____

7. Would a country have a **boarder** or **border**? _____

8. Would dinosaur bones be found at a **cite** or **site**? _____

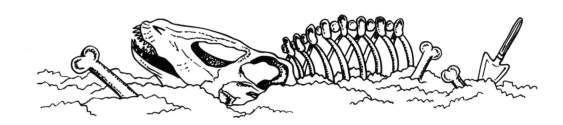

9. Would horses be kept in a **chorale** or **corral**? _____

10. Would a plane be stored in a **hangar** or **hanger**? _____

11. Would a pencil have **led** or **lead**? _____

12. Would you learn a **lesson** or **lessen**? _____

13. Would grass be **mode** or **mowed**? _____

14. Would you get a bargain at a **sale** or **sail**? _____

15. Would a skunk have a **sent** or **scent**? _____

16. Would an apartment be **least** or **leased**? _____

17. Would you write on **stationary** or **stationery**? _____

Directions: Study each pair of homonyms, then read the sentence and the meanings below. Decide which meaning applies to the sentence and fill in the bubble. Then write the correct word in the blank. Be careful—these are purposely tricky.

peek *peak*   1. We looked out over the valley from the _____ .
  O a quick look or glance   O the summit or top

patience *patients*   2. Being a nurse takes a lot of _____.
  O composure; forbearing   O those under medical care

assistance *assistants*   3. Students work as _____ in the computer lab.
  O help; aid   O people who help or aid

weather *whether*   4. I wonder _____ it will rain or not.
  O precipitation, temperature   O if

straight *strait*   5. The ship was on course, heading _____ to the island.
  O directly; not crooked   O a narrow channel of water

pedal *peddle*   6. The old man tried to _____ used bike parts.
  O foot rest; pump feet to move   O sell

overdo *overdue*   7. Not again! I just realized my library book is _____.
  O do too much   O late

through *threw*   8. The player was able to dunk the ball _____ the hoop.
  O in and out of; finished   O tossed; hurled

vein *vain*   9. The doctor made a _____ attempt to give my dog a shot.
  O a blood vessel   O futile; fruitless; unsuccessful

pause *paws*   10. I had to _____ when I spotted the injured animal.
  O a brief stop   O feet of animals

NAME _____   DATE _____

Directions: These homonyms are among the most troublesome—not just for students, but for many adults. (Watch for incorrect use of these words on signs, flyers, and TV and Internet ads!) Study the meanings carefully, then apply them by writing the correct words in the blanks.

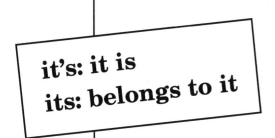

it's: it is
its: belongs to it

1. You can't judge a book by _____ cover.

2. I think _____ going to be a sunny weekend.

3. The moon doesn't give off _____ own light.

4. What is _____ main purpose?

5. I never knew _____ name.

6. Is that _____ best friend?

7. What is _____ favorite team?

8. It looks like _____ going to be late.

9. I think _____ getting taller every day!

10. It is _____ turn to go first.

you're: you are
your: belongs to you

who's: who is
whose: belongs to who

11. I wonder _____ moving in next door.

12. Dad asked _____ coat was in the hall.

13. We don't know _____ in charge.

14. I wondered _____ class I would be in.

15. It's my sister _____ always on the phone.

16. I heard that _____ identical twins.

17. I think _____ repaving the road soon.

18. Dogs must remain with _____ owners.

19. I lost _____ address.

20. Some children forgot _____ permission slips.

they're: they are
their: belongs to them

NAME _____   DATE _____

Directions: The pairs of words below are not homonyms but are very frequently confused. See if you can spot the impostors below. Follow the directions for each part.

A. *Match each word to its definition. If necessary, consult a dictionary to be sure.*

1. **lose**: _____

   loose: _____

2. **of**: _____

   off: _____

3. **than**: _____

   then: _____

4. **affect**: _____

   effect: _____

5. **accept**: _____

   except: _____

6. **conscience**: _____

   conscious: _____

agree to; take
exclude; leave out
not tight
misplace; not win
not on; drop away from
relating to
sense of right and wrong
aware; awake
at that time; next
compared with
influence; cause
result; consequence

B. *The sentences below contain incorrect words. Is the sentence correct as is, or does it contain an impostor? Write ✓ (correct) or ✗ (impostor). Then underline any imposter words you find.*

____ 1. Please except my apology.

____ 2. A button came off my shirt.

____ 3. I was conscious of his presence.

____ 4. She is older then I am.

____ 5. The dog ran lose in the yard.

____ 6. Everyone went accept Bob.

____ 7. Did the rain affect their plans?

____ 8. He stopped then turned around.

____ 9. Extra credit will effect your grade.

____ 10. I accept your invitation to the party.

____ 11. Jupiter is much larger then Earth.

____ 12. You are almost out off time.

____ 13. Don't loose those tickets!

____ 14. I brushed than flossed my teeth.

____ 15. The volcano had a devastating effect.

____ 16. She had a guilty conscious.

Signal words or phrases provide clues about what is coming. They help you focus on what is to follow and be ready to understand it.

Directions: Use the options in the signs to answer what you think would follow the 15 phrases below (the first one has been done for you).

AN EXAMPLE OR LIST

A COMPARISON OR OPPOSING IDEA

AN IMPORTANT POINT

MORE IDEAS WILL FOLLOW

A CONCLUSION

1. **as a result**... ___A conclusion___

2. **for instance**... _____

3. **and finally**... _____

4. **on the other hand**... _____

5. **such as**... _____

6. **furthermore**... _____

7. **conversely**... _____

8. **although**... _____

9. **in summary**... _____

10. **however**... _____

11. **in contrast**... _____

12. **specifically**... _____

13. **a key feature**... _____

14. **yet**... _____

15. **in the final analysis**... _____

Learning the meaning of abbreviations by heart will help you breeze past them while reading just as you do with whole words.

Directions: An abbreviation is a shortened form of a word or phrase. They are used extensively in a variety of types of writing. Making up your own for personal communication can be W. C. (way cool), but you need to know the standard ones below. Test yourself now. Write out the full word for each abbreviation.

1. Ave. _____

2. ea. _____

3. dept. _____

4. amt. _____

5. Wed. _____

6. Dr. _____

7. cm _____

8. qt. _____

9. yr. _____

10. Gov. _____

11. Sept. _____

12. oz. _____

13. Mr. _____

14. wk. _____

15. Rd. _____

16. Dec. _____

17. Blvd. _____

18. doz. _____

19. Capt. _____

20. Tues. _____

21. gal. _____

22. St. _____

23. Oct. _____

24. Mt. _____

25. Rte. _____

26. ft. _____

27. Fri. _____

28. Jr. _____

29. Hwy. _____

30. m.p.h. _____

CHALLENGER: Write the abbreviations for these words:

31. et cetera _____

32. world wide web _____

33. miscellaneous _____

A good way to get a basic understanding of a story is to look for the answers to the 5 Ws: who, what, where, when, and why.

Directions: News stories are often written based on the 5 Ws. The historical event described below is written as a news story. Answer the questions to identify the 5 Ws.

DAILY HERALD

Saturday, April 15, 1865 Yesterday was indeed a sad day for Americans. After bearing the weight of a long and bloody war, our President was finally feeling optimistic about reuniting the country. He had plans to bring the South back into the Union fold and rebuild our wounded nation. After meeting with his Cabinet, Lincoln took a much-needed break by escorting his wife and another couple to Ford's Theater to see the play *Our American Cousin*. Apparently, the Washington police man assigned to guard the President either left his post or was distracted just long enough for a person to shoot a pistol. Lincoln slumped in his seat. A man leaped from the President's box and in the confusion was able to escape through a back exit. A witness claims that the man shouted, "The South shall live!" but one thing is for sure—Abraham Lincoln did not.

1. **Who** is the subject of the story? _____

2. **What** event is the story about? _____

_____

3. **Where** did the event take place? _____

_____

4. **When** did the event happen? _____

5. **Why** did this event occur? _____

_____

CHALLENGERS! Now apply what you have learned about the 5 Ws.

1. Choose another historical event. Research it, then use the 5 Ws to write it as a news story.

2. Find a current events article in a recent newspaper. Identify the 5 Ws.

NAME _____   DATE _____

Directions: Hey—you don't read just stories and text, you read plenty of other stuff, too, such as ads. An ad is designed to interest you in buying or doing something. In order to accomplish that, the ad must give you the information you need. How? The 5 Ws!
Read the ad below. Identify the 5 Ws. (P.S. This is not real.)

Hey Football Fans... **WOULDN'T YOU LIKE TO SHOW YOUR SPIRIT BY WEARING A REPLICA OF YOUR FAVORITE PLAYER'S JERSEY?**

If you order now, you can be wearing your jersey for the opening game. But hurry, this is a limited time offer. You must order by August to receive your jersey in time for the season opener in September. Just choose your favorite NFL team and player's name, tell us what size (S, M, L, XL), pay just $49.95 plus $5.95 shipping & handling, and your jersey will be on its way. You should receive it in 7-10 days. Offer ends Aug. 31.

Don't Delay or your team's jersey may be sold out! Order NOW by phone or online at our Web site.

FANtastic Replicas, Inc. • **2291 Your St.** • **Any Town, CA 00009**
1•800•000•0000   www.anyfan.com

Part 1: The Basic 5

1. **Who** is the advertiser? _____

2. **What** does the ad want you to buy? _____

3. **Where** can you buy it? _____

_____

4. **When** will the offer end? _____

5. **Why** does the advertiser say you should buy it? _____

_____

Part 2: More Ws

6. **Who** is the ad directed toward? _____

7. **What** is the price? _____

8. **When** will you receive your purchase? _____

9. **Why** should you buy it now? _____

Directions: You use the 5 Ws to get basic information from what you read. You can also use them to give information. Design an invitation to a party you'd like to have. Tell who is giving it, what kind of party it is, where it is being held, when it is, and why it's happening. Add any other information the invitee would need or like. Then decorate your invitation to go with the type of party you chose.

Who: _____

What: _____

_____

_____

Where: _____

_____

When: _____

Why: _____

_____

_____

From the time you learned your ABCs you have been using sequence as a reading tool.

Directions: Below is an edited excerpt from *Alice In Wonderland* by Lewis Carroll. After you read it, number the events in the order that they happened. Beware, one event didn't happen at all. Put an ✗ on that line instead of a number.

By this time Alice had found her way into a tidy little room with a table in the window, and on it (as she had hoped) a fan and two or three pairs of tiny white kid-gloves. She took up the fan and a pair of the gloves, and was just going to leave the room when her eye fell upon a little bottle that stood near the looking-glass. There was no label this time with the words DRINK ME, but nevertheless she uncorked it and put it to her lips. "I know something *interesting* is sure to happen," she said to herself, "whenever I eat or drink anything: so I'll just see what this bottle does. I do hope it'll make me grow again, for really, I'm quite tired of being such a tiny thing."

It did so indeed, and much sooner that she had expected. Before she had drunk half the bottle, she found her head pressing against the ceiling, and had to stoop to save her neck from being broken. She hastily put down the bottle, saying to herself, "I hope I shan't grow any more. As it is, I can't get out the door. I do wish I hadn't drunk so much."

Alas! It was too late to wish that! She kept on growing, and growing, and very soon had to kneel down on the floor. In another minute there was not even room for this, and...still she kept on growing, putting one arm out the window, and one foot up the chimney, saying to herself, "Now I can do no more....What will become of me?"

_____ Alice stooped to keep from breaking her neck.

_____ Alice stopped drinking from the bottle.

_____ Alice found a bottle marked DRINK ME.

_____ Alice put her foot up the chimney.

_____ Alice spotted a little bottle near the looking-glass.

_____ Alice hoped the drink would make her grow.

_____ Alice found a fan and gloves.

_____ Alice wished she hadn't drunk so much.

_____ Alice found her way into a tidy little room.

Directions: Sequence is an important part of following directions. Below are the directions for making a pipe-cleaner animal. But they are out of order, and so are the illustrations. First, number the figures in order from 1–6. Then write the directions in the order.

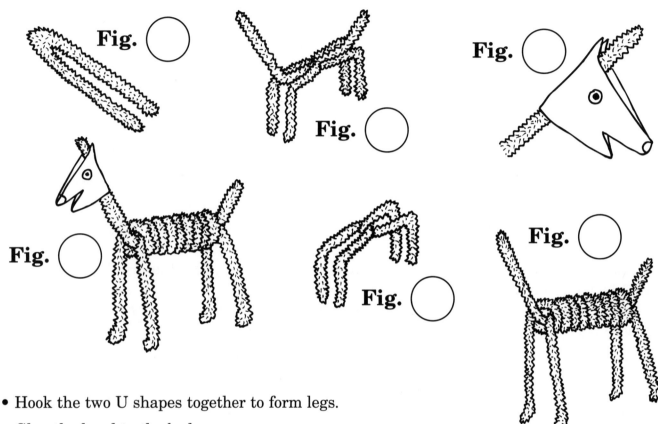

Fig. ◯   Fig. ◯   Fig. ◯   Fig. ◯   Fig. ◯   Fig. ◯

- Hook the two U shapes together to form legs.
- Glue the head to the body.
- Bend two pipe cleaners into U shapes.
- Make a head from folded cardboard.
- Bend another pipe cleaner up at the ends to form head and tail.
- Twist a fourth pipe cleaner around the body.

1. _____

2. _____

3. _____

4. _____

5. _____

6. _____

CHALLENGER! Make a spider from pipe cleaners. Then write the directions for how to make it.

Directions: Being comfortable with alphabetizing makes it easier to find what you want in a dictionary, thesaurus, or encyclopedia. Here is a fun way to practice!

A. *Match each word on the left to its meaning on the right. Write its letter on the line.*

____ 1. **incredible**   A. command; legal order

____ 2. **recline**   B. something that annoys, troubles, or offends

____ 3. **novelty**   C. useful tool, instrument, or utensil

____ 4. **implement**   D. extraordinary; beyond belief

____ 5. **smitten**   E. bring or come together; recover

____ 6. **rally**   F. a new or unusual thing

____ 7. **mandate**   G. to lean back or lie down

____ 8. **nuisance**   H. keep away from; avoid

____ 9. **shun**   I. struck; hit hard

B. *To solve the puzzle, write the words above in alphabetical order, one letter to a blank. Then read the word under the ★. Fill it in the blank to complete the sentence.*

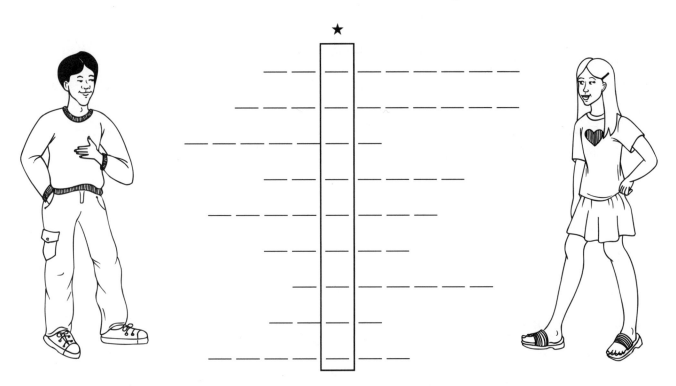

Computers are now _____ in homes as well as in offices.

(widespread, common, in general use)

Directions: Reading your own writing—peice of cake, right? (Did you catch that typo?) Be sure to include proofreading into set of reading skills. Here's a puzzle that will help you spot words frequently misspelled because the letters are not in the correct order.

One word in each sentence is written with the wrong letter sequence. Find the misspelled word. Write it correctly in the puzzle.

ACROSS

5. I laughed becuase it was funny.

6. This is gauranteed to be fun.

9. Those flowers are beuatiful.

11. Did you recieve my letter?

13. Please be queit during the movie.

14. It made me niether happy nor sad.

15. Danny siad he was coming by.

DOWN

1. This is not a conveneint time.

2. May I have a peice of pie?

3. Thunderclouds began to rumbel.

4. Let's eat at a restuarant.

7. Koalas are my favorite aminal.

8. May I borrow a nickle?

10. Abby is my best freind.

12. This is my frist time flying alone.

For something to be fact it must be true for everyone and in all cases. Otherwise it could just be someone's opinion.

Directions: Chocolate is delicious. Fact or opinion? You may agree, and it may even be true for most people, but it is not true for everyone in all cases. It is an opinion. Don't mistake opinions you agree with for facts. Practice this below.

1. Roller coasters are fun.

    O This is a fact.

    O This is an opinion and I agree.

    O This is an opinion and I disagree.

2. Baby animals are cute.

    O This is a fact.

    O This is an opinion and I agree.

    O This is an opinion and I disagree.

3. Most snakes are not poisonous.

    O This is a fact.

    O This is an opinion and I agree.

    O This is an opinion and I disagree.

4. The sun is a star.

    O This is a fact.

    O This is an opinion and I agree.

    O This is an opinion and I disagree.

5. It's important to eat breakfast.

    O This is a fact.

    O This is an opinion and I agree.

    O This is an opinion and I disagree.

6. Learning to skate is easy.

    O This is a fact.

    O This is an opinion and I agree.

    O This is an opinion and I disagree.

7. A moose is from the deer family.

    O This is a fact.

    O This is an opinion and I agree.

    O This is an opinion and I disagree.

8. You should recycle cans and bottles.

    O This is a fact.

    O This is an opinion and I agree.

    O This is an opinion and I disagree.

9. Listening to music is enjoyable.

    O This is a fact.

    O This is an opinion and I agree.

    O This is an opinion and I disagree.

10. Egypt is in Africa.

    O This is a fact.

    O This is an opinion and I agree.

    O This is an opinion and I disagree.

CHALLENGER: Judgment words, such as *pretty* or *shouldn't*, are clues that a statement may be an opinion. List the six words in the statements above that let you know they were opinions:

_____

_____

NAME _____   DATE _____

Directions: Separate fact from opinion. Highlight any sentence that is an opinion in the passages below.

A. The main function of your teeth is to tear, grind, and chew your food. But, a healthy smile is desirable, too. A dentist is a type of doctor that specializes in caring for your teeth. Becoming a dentist takes years of schooling and special training. It is hard work. You should visit a dentist twice a year. He or she can check your teeth for decay or other problems. The dentist can fill any cavities you may have, recommend that you get braces, or suggest other procedures. But seeing a dentist will not ensure that your teeth stay healthy and strong. Good dental health is up to you. Brushing every day is essential, but it is not enough. Flossing is important, too. And, don't forget the critical role a balanced diet plays in overall health, including your teeth.

B. K-9 is a clever name used to identify specially-trained police dogs, or canines. Only the most intelligent breeds are worthy of becoming police dogs. German shepherds are most prevalent, but other breeds, such as the Belgian Malinois, are also used. When

assigned to an officer, a police dog becomes his or her companion and partner. The dog may be called upon to sniff out illegal substances, stop a suspect from running away, or protect its master from attack. A police dog is the greatest friend an officer can have. Both the officer and the dog enjoy the close bond that forms. But, more importantly, the officer relies on the dog for his or her safety on the job. Dogs are loyal creatures, but K-9's are far beyond that. Many have given their lives in the line of duty. And they, like their fellow officers, are ceremoniously honored.

Your brain can make sense of all sorts of information that it receives. Two great organizing tools you use are categorizing and classifying.

Directions: On the left is a list of feelings. Sort them into the categories shown. Then, draw an expression on each face to represent the category.

hostile
delighted
admiration
capable
aggravated
apprehensive
anxious
considerate
amused
irritated
dejected
assured
suspicious
enraged
affectionate
exuberant
glum
uneasy
effective
forlorn
despondent
gratified
devoted
skillful

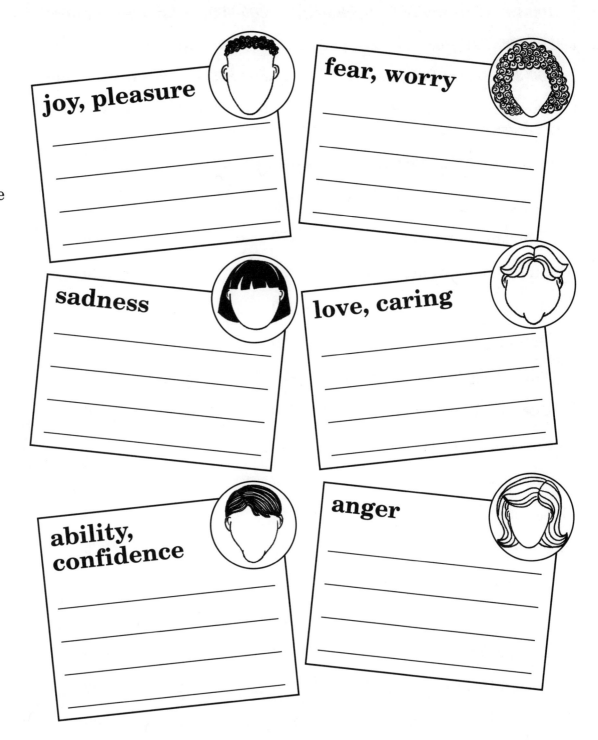

joy, pleasure

fear, worry

sadness

love, caring

ability, confidence

anger

NAME _____   DATE _____

Directions: Even though you can surf the net to find almost any information, you still want to know how to navigate the library. The books in the library are classified by the Dewey Decimal System. Get acquainted with them below.

000-999 Generalities	*500-599 Natural Science & Mathematics*
100-199 Philosophy & Psychology	*600-699 Technology (Applied Sciences)*
200-299 Religion	*700-799 The Arts*
300-399 Social Sciences	*800-899 Literature & Rhetoric*
400-499 Language	*900-999 Geography & History*

Circle the number that shows where each topic would be classified in the Dewey Decimal System.

A. Paintings of Van Gogh	750	540	280
B. Comparative Religion	170	290	530
C. Ethics (moral values)	090	570	170
D. World Travel	910	430	820
E. Greek Myths	880	640	050
F. Traditional Japanese Customs	720	390	620
G. Chemical Engineering	430	910	660
H. Supreme Court Decisions	340	610	450
I. The Bible	220	740	650
J. General Library Science	940	020	760
K. Photography	330	570	770
L. Astronomy	520	840	090
M. Linguistics	410	510	960
N. Zoological Sciences	460	850	590
O. Mental Health	530	300	150
P. Stringed Instruments	950	780	330
Q. Agricultural Technology	140	630	460

NAME _____   DATE _____

Directions: There are around ten million species of animals. Zoologists use a special system to classify them using Latin and Greek words. Learn about animal classification by studying the example. Then use the table to answer the questions.

KINGDOM — ANIMALIA (animal)

PHYLUM — CHORDATA (animal with backbone)

CLASS — MAMMALIA (animal w/ backbone that nurses its young)

ORDER — RODENTIA (animal w/ backbone, nurses young & has sharp teeth)

FAMILY — SCIURIDAE (animal w/ backbone, nurses young, has sharp teeth & a bushy tail)

GENUS — TAMIASCIURUS (animal w/ backbone, nurses young, has sharp teeth, bushy tail, & climbs trees)

SPECIES — HUDSONICUS (animal w/ backbone, nurses young, has sharp teeth, bushy tail, climbs trees, & brown fur)

	Mystery Animal "A"	Mystery Animal "B"	Mystery Animal "C"	Mystery Animal "D"
KINGDOM	ANIMALIA	ANIMALIA	ANIMALIA	ANIMALIA
PHYLUM	CHORDATA	CHORDATA	CHORDATA	ARTHROPODA
CLASS	MAMMALIA	MAMMALIA	AVES	CRUSTACEA
ORDER	CARNIVORA	CETACEA	FALCONIFORMES	DECAPODA
FAMILY	URSIDAE	BALAENOPTERIDAE	ACCIPITRIDAE	COENOBITIDAE
GENUS	AILUROPODA	BALAENOPTERA	HALIAEETUS	COENOBITA
SPECIES	AILUROPODA MELANOLEUCA	BALAENOPTERA MUSCULUS	HALIAEETUS LEUCOCEPHALUS	COENOBITA PERLATUS

1. Which mystery animal does not have a backbone? _____

2. Think about the word *aviation*. Which mystery animal is a bird? _____

3. A cetacean is a large water animal. Could animal "B" be a fish? _____

4. In Latin *deca* means ten and *pod* means foot. Could animal "D" be a snail? _____

5. There are two kinds of whales—toothed and baleen. Could animal "B" be a whale? _____

6. In Latin, the Big Dipper is Ursa Major, or Big Bear. Which mystery animal is a bear? ____

7. How many of the mystery animals nurse their young? _____

8. Which mystery animal has a shell? _____

CHALLENGER: Identify each mystery animal:

bald eagle _____   giant panda _____   hermit crab ____   blue whale _____

Some things just always go together—like cause and effect. Remember that the cause is the reason and the effect is the result.

Directions: Read this tongue-in-cheek news story based on a well-known fairy tale. Then match cause to effect.

BOY COMES INTO "GIANT" FORTUNE

Taletown—A boy and his mother no longer have to live in poverty. After disappointing his mother by not selling the cow as he was asked to do in order that they not starve, Jack more than made up for his delinquency by acquiring a goose that lays golden eggs.

Instead of selling the cow, Jack traded it for some magic beans. When he handed his mother the beans instead of cash, she threw them out the window and sent Jack to bed without supper. The next morning a huge beanstalk had grown all the way to the sky. Being curious, as children are, Jack climbed the beanstalk. At the top he found a giant who owned quite a bit of valuable stuff,

"Stalking" a Fortune

the best of which, Jack surmised, was a goose that laid golden eggs. With some effort and because he was a clever boy, Jack was able to grab the goose and escape down the beanstalk. As soon as he hit the ground, he chopped it down to prevent the giant from reclaiming the hen or taking retribution on Jack.

So now, the formerly poor boy and his mother live in luxury, thanks to a giant reversal of fortune.

CAUSE (reason)	**EFFECT** (result)
1. Jack and his mother had no money, so	he traded the cow for them.
2. Jack was enticed by the magic beans, so	he climbed the beanstalk.
3. Jack did not sell the cow as told, so	mother sent Jack to sell the cow.
4. Mother was angry about getting beans, so	she threw them out the window
5. Jack was curious, so	he was able to grab the goose and escape.
6. Jack was a clever boy, so	he and his mother live in luxury.
7. Jack didn't want the giant to catch him, so	he chopped down the beanstalk.
8. Jack acquired a golden goose, so	Jack was sent to bed without supper.

Directions: There's a reason for everything, they say. Another way to put this is, when something happens, there's a cause for it. A cause sets up circumstances for a result to occur. That result is the effect of the cause. Use your imagination below to speculate what might have been the cause or effect in the circumstances below.

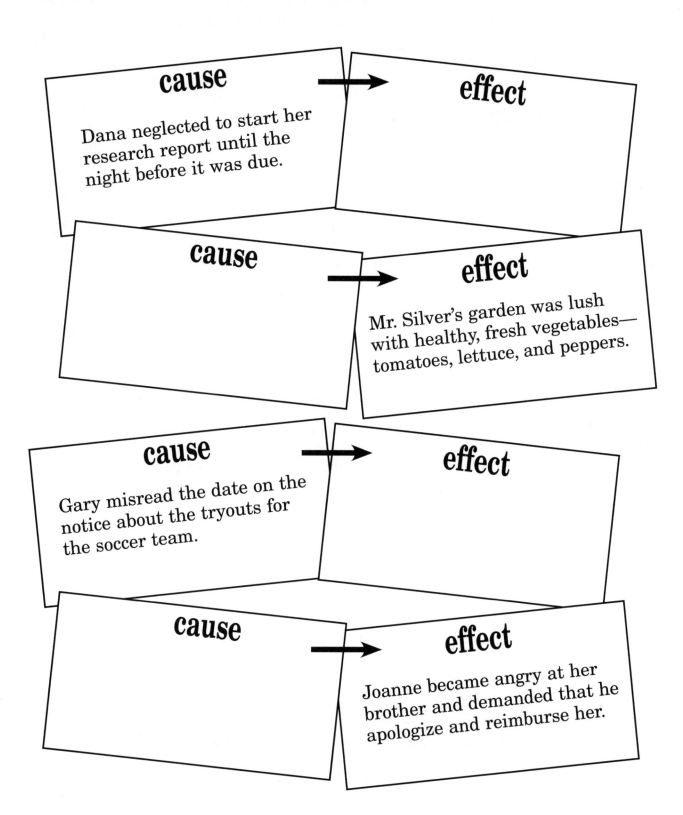

cause → effect

Dana neglected to start her research report until the night before it was due.

cause → effect

Mr. Silver's garden was lush with healthy, fresh vegetables—tomatoes, lettuce, and peppers.

cause → effect

Gary misread the date on the notice about the tryouts for the soccer team.

cause → effect

Joanne became angry at her brother and demanded that he apologize and reimburse her.

In reading, the "point" of a story is the main idea. Being able to recognize it is a good strategy.

Directions: Read each group of three sentences. Decide which is the main idea and which are details that support it. Then write main idea or detail in front of each sentence.

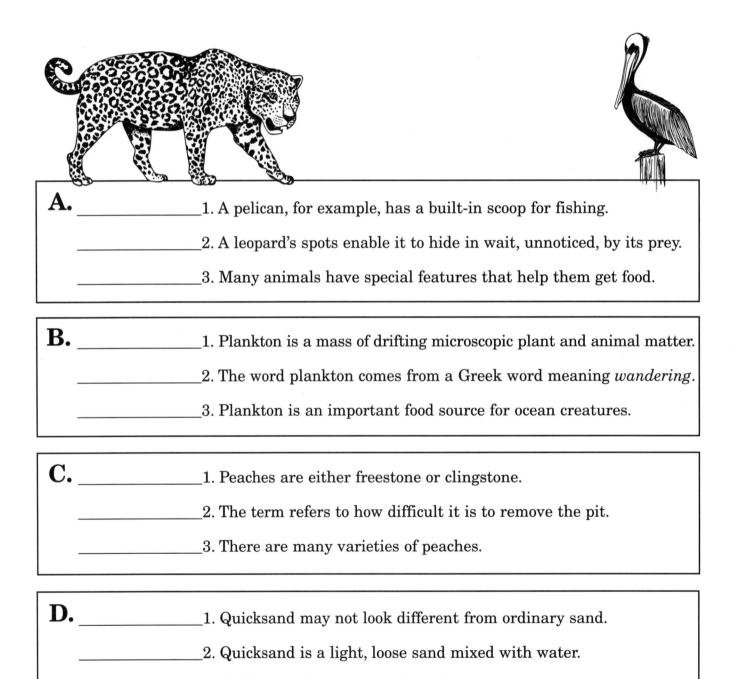

A. _____ 1. A pelican, for example, has a built-in scoop for fishing.

_____ 2. A leopard's spots enable it to hide in wait, unnoticed, by its prey.

_____ 3. Many animals have special features that help them get food.

B. _____ 1. Plankton is a mass of drifting microscopic plant and animal matter.

_____ 2. The word plankton comes from a Greek word meaning *wandering*.

_____ 3. Plankton is an important food source for ocean creatures.

C. _____ 1. Peaches are either freestone or clingstone.

_____ 2. The term refers to how difficult it is to remove the pit.

_____ 3. There are many varieties of peaches.

D. _____ 1. Quicksand may not look different from ordinary sand.

_____ 2. Quicksand is a light, loose sand mixed with water.

_____ 3. Unlike regular sand, quicksand cannot support weight.

Directions: As you read the paragraph about Pompeii, think about the main idea of the passage, the relevant details, and what doesn't belong there. Then answer the questions below.

Pompeii

The word Pompeii brings to mind a picture of a city buried in volcanic ash and the inhabitants caught frozen in time. But, when Mount Vesuvius erupted in A.D. 79, engulfing the city of Pompeii, most of the people escaped. It must have been a very frightening experience. Though they did not have much time, many were able to carry off their most valuable, moveable possessions to safety. Later, when the eruption was over, some people tunneled back into buildings to remove even more. The excavation of Pompeii is of immense importance, not for the objects of value left behind, but for the incredible information it provides about how the people of that time lived.

1. This paragraph is meant to be factual. Write the sentence that is an opinion and does not belong. _____

2. Which of the following would be the best title for this passage: Instant Destruction, Frozen in Time, The Real Value of Pompeii? _____

3. Is the main idea of a paragraph always the first sentence? _____

4. Why were few personal objects of value found in the excavation of Pompeii? _____
   _____

5. Choose the sentence that best states the main idea of the paragraph:
   a. The inhabitants of Pompeii were frightened.
   b. Mount Vesuvius erupted in A.D. 79.
   c. Some people escaped before the city was buried.
   d. The excavation of Pompeii is of great historical importance.
   e. Excavators were disappointed that few valuable objects were found.

Directions: In December of 1938, something amazing happened. Read about it, then answer the questions.

It was December 22, 1938. A fishing boat was out trawling in choppy waters near the southern tip of the African peninsula. Some fishermen had just pulled in a full net of fish. Spreading the catch out on deck, several kinds of fish flopped around on the planks. One odd-looking one caught the eye of the fishermen. They noted that it was nearly the length of a man, five feet or so, and must have weighed over 100 pounds. It had heavy scales and big bulging eyes. A bit of a hubbub ensued and the skipper came down to see what the commotion was about. No one, not even the most experienced seaman, had ever seen such a creature. It was huge and ugly. It didn't look edible and some wanted to just throw it overboard. But the skipper stopped them. They hauled it back to land, where some scientists examined it. It was not unknown to them.
Paleontologists knew of it from fossilized rock. It was a coelacanth, believed to have become extinct along with the dinosaurs sixty-five million years ago. Yet, here it was, in the flesh. The discovery of the coelacanth was proof that if one species had survived undetected for millions of years, perhaps others have as well.

1. This paragraph is meant to be factual. Write the sentence that is an opinion and does not belong. _____

2. Which of the following would be the best title for this passage: Presumed Dead, Out of Extinction, An Unexpected Catch? _____

3. Based on context clues, what do these words mean? choppy: _____
   trawling: _____ hubbub: _____

4. Was coelacanth discovered in the Northern or Southern Hemisphere? _____

5. Choose the sentence that best states the main idea of the paragraph:

   a. The coelacanth was not edible.

   b. It's a good thing they didn't toss the fish overboard.

   c. The discovery of the coelacanth raised questions about species assumed extinct.

   d. Paleontologists were already familiar with the coelacanth and recognized it.

   e. Experienced seamen can tell which fish are worth saving and which are not.

Directions: A fiction story can also have a main idea. Read the story, then answer the questions.

"I said no, Denise, and I mean it."

"But Mom..."

I held the little kitten in my arms. He mewed like a doll.

"Look, Mom—he's soooo cute."

"He also probably has fleas, needs shots, and...CUTE does not pay for these things. Are you going to? Even if you could pay the vet bill, which you can't, there is still the cost of feeding him every day and other expenses. You don't realize how much it costs to have a pet. We simply can't afford to add another one right now."

I hung my head and looked as dejected as I possibly could. It didn't work. So I tried another approach.

"We can't just leave him in the street to fend for himself! He'd die!"

There was silence and for a moment I thought the guilt angle was working. I waited.

"Here's what we can do—make that what YOU can do. Call your Aunt Sylvia. She lives alone and may enjoy the company of a pet, and I know that she can afford it. But, if she doesn't want to adopt this stray, get back on the phone and call everyone you know who might be willing. Someone will take him. He can stay on the porch until you find him a home."

At this point I knew I had lost. So, I called Aunt Sylvia. I didn't even have to use the sympathy or the guilt play. She actually said she had been thinking about getting a cat and would be happy to have it.

"And, of course, Denise, you may come by any time to visit us."

Well, maybe I didn't lose after all.

1. Choose the sentence that best summarizes the main idea of the story.

       a. Parents often have to base decisions on financial circumstances.

       b. Kids do not make enough money to support having pets.

       c. It is important to find a stray a good home.

2. True or false? Denise's mom did not care what happened to the stray. _____

3. What two emotions did Denise try to illicit from her mom in order to get her to change her mind about keeping the stray cat? _____ and

_____

4. Which of the following do you think Denise's mom values most highly: taking responsibility, pleasing others, or not wasting money? _____

_____

5. Copy the sentence that tells you whether or not Denise already had a pet. _____

_____

Directions: This is a fiction story, but you may still learn some interesting facts.

I like astronomy and all that, but some things used to confuse me. For example, I had never been able to get clear on eclipses. I read about them and still I was not straight about the difference between a solar eclipse and a lunar eclipse.

A visit by a friend of my father's changed all that. Dr. Fielding is a college professor who went to school with my dad way back in the early 70s. He came over for dinner one evening, and we got to talking about my interest in astronomy, and specifically, my confusion about eclipses. That's when Dr. Fielding cleared it all up for me.

The word eclipse means that something is being hidden in the shadow of something else. A specific eclipse is named for the thing that is being hidden, or obscured. So, on a sunny day, if I stand in front of my dog, Rusty, so that I am between him and the light and my shadow falls on him, it is a "Rusty eclipse." (OK, I made that up, but it helps me understand better.) The word sol means sun, and in a solar eclipse, the view of sun is being obscured by the moon. Luna means moon, and of course, in a lunar eclipse, it is the moon that is obscured, this time by the shadow of the Earth.

Hey, if you were confused about eclipses, too, but now you get it, I'll thank Dr. Fielding for you.

1. Summarize in your own words the main idea of the story. _____

_____

2. In a total solar eclipse, what object can you not see? _____

3. In a lunar eclipse, what is causing the shadow? _____

4. The author chose a personal and informal tone. Do you think this was an effective way to present scientific information? _____ Why or why not? _____

_____

5. Cite two examples of informal, casual language used in the story: _____

_____

NAME _____   DATE _____

Directions: Using the sentences below, write a paragraph that compares spiders to insects.
Note: You will not use three of the sentences; mark them with an ✗.

TOPIC: Compare spiders to insects.

_____ Though many people think of spiders as insects, they are not.

_____ Scientists classify spiders as arachnids, which have four pairs of legs and two body parts.

_____ Insects, on the other hand, generally have three body parts and three pairs of legs.

_____ Some spiders are poisonous, but most are harmless.

_____ As arachnids, spiders are more closely related to scorpions than to insects.

_____ The black widow is one of the few spiders dangerous to people.

_____ Another difference is the presence or absence of antennae.

_____ Spiders do not have antennae.

_____ A spider can have two, four, six, or eight eyes.

_____ Spiders can also do something no insect can—weave webs.

_____ One thing spiders and insects do have in common—they are plentiful almost everywhere.

_____

_____

_____

_____

_____

_____

_____

_____

_____

_____

_____

_____

_____

Directions: Match the sentences to the correct topic and write them on the lines provided. Ignore the sentence that has nothing to do with either topic.

I. TOPIC: The Geography of Egypt

_____

_____

_____

_____

_____

II. TOPIC: The History of Egypt

_____

_____

_____

_____

_____

Arabic is the predominant language in Egypt.

Egypt is a nation in northeastern Africa.

It covers an area of about 386,000 square miles.

The region that is now Egypt has been civilized since prehistoric times.

Most of the country is covered by dry, windswept desert.

Cairo University is the largest of Egypt's public universities.

The Nile River provides most of the water for the country.

Great cities and kingdoms date back to at least 3100 B.C.

The vast majority of the people live in the fertile Nile River basin.

The arid conditions have preserved many of Egypt's historical sites.

Many tourists visit Egypt yearly.

Great temples and mummies of pharaohs are among its ancient treasures.

Directions: Compare two ways to organize information by topic and subtopic: a map and an outline. Study the map below, then fill in the missing topics where they belong on the corresponding outline.

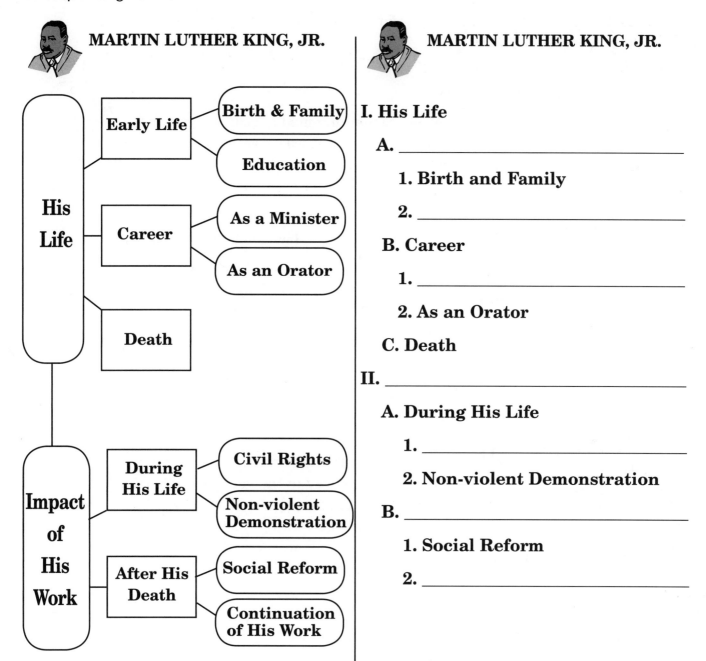

MARTIN LUTHER KING, JR.

I. His Life

  A. _____

    1. Birth and Family

    2. _____

  B. Career

    1. _____

    2. As an Orator

  C. Death

II. _____

  A. During His Life

    1. _____

    2. Non-violent Demonstration

  B. _____

    1. Social Reform

    2. _____

Which of the two ways to organize information, map or outline, do you prefer and why?

_____

_____

Reading can be tricky. Sometimes information is not given directly. You have to use clues to draw conclusions and inferences.

Directions: In the two situations below, look for what is not directly stated but can be concluded or inferred from clues given.

A. The alarm went off at 6:30 as usual. Something made Trish look out the window. It was just as she had hoped. The street was covered, the trees were barely visible, and nothing was moving in the white stillness. There would be no school today!

1. Was it 6:30 a.m. or 6:30 p.m.? _____ How do you know? _____
   _____

2. What had happened during the night? _____

3. What sentence gives you a clue that Trish had anticipated what happened? _____
   _____

B. Jerome spoke softly to Petey, but it was of no use. He squawked all the way to the vet. Jerome carried Petey's cage inside, and Petey screamed every word he knew at the dogs and cats in the waiting room. The vet put on gloves and checked Petey all over. He then pronounced him fit as a fiddle and said, "See ya next year, Pete."

1. Was specific type of pet do you think Petey is and why? _____
   _____

2. Why did the vet use gloves when handling Petey?_____

3. Did Petey visit the vet for a routine exam or because he was injured? _____
   How do you know? _____

Directions: Read about the Sanchez family. Think about what is not stated directly in the information given. Then answer the questions.

The Sanchez Family

Grandma   Grandpa   Carlo   Marie   Junior   Leann   Laura   Billy   Mark

1. Grandpa's name is Joe Sanchez. Is he Carlo's or Marie's father? _____
   How can you tell? _____

2. Leann and Laura are sisters and the same age. How can that be? _____
   _____

3. Junior just got his driver's license. Can you conclude how old he is? _____ Why or
   why not? _____

4. Leann and Laura are in the eighth grade. Can you conclude that Junior is older than
   they are? _____ Why or why not? _____

5. Grandma Sanchez watches the two youngest children while the rest of the family is at
   work and school. Who does she babysit? _____
   How can you tell? _____

6. After work, Carlo picks up the boys at Grandma's and gets dinner started. Does
   Grandma live with the Sanchez family? _____ How do you know? _____
   _____

7. All the Sanchez children have jobs around the house. Even Mark feeds the fish. What
   can you conclude about the parents or children from this? _____
   _____

   Feeding and cleaning up after Bucky is Junior's job. Can you conclude that Bucky is a
   dog? _____ Why or why not? _____

Directions: Read the sentences below, then fill in the circle of the correct answer drawing conclustions from what you have read.

1. "Take it for a test drive. I think you will be very pleased with the performance."

   O An actor

   O A car salesman

   O An antique dealer

2. "Looks as if your main line is clogged. I'll have to snake it."

   O A zoologist

   O An electrician

   O A plumber

3. "I have added special supports to the building plan to ensure that it is structurally sound."

   O An architect

   O An archaeologist

   O A computer technician

4. "Please write your account number on this deposit slip."

   O A veterinarian

   O A bank teller

   O A truck driver

5. "Remember, your research reports on ancient Greece are due on Friday."

   O A social studies teacher

   O A travel agent

   O A librarian

6. "The piece I have acquired will make a nice addition to our collection."

   O An artist

   O A talent scout

   O A museum curator

7. "This area is very dry right now. Be extra careful with fire during your camp-out."

   O A forest ranger

   O A groundskeeper

   O A sports coach

8. "I think next season I will be able to put corn in that fallow field."

   O A horse rancher

   O A farmer

   O A pharmacist

9. "Your logo should be prominent as well as your phone number and web address."

   O A police officer

   O A photographer

   O An ad designer

10. "There is no evidence of termites, but the roof needs repairs in several sections."

   O A house inspector

   O A real estate agent

   O A exterminator

NAME _____ DATE _____

Directions: After each description below, write two things you can infer from it. Remember, an inference is something you can conclude without being told directly.

A.

As he walks toward the building, Tony is irritated with himself. In one arm are three books. His other hand jingles the change in his pocket. "If I had not been so forgetful, I could have used this money for something instead of having to pay a fine."

1. Where is Tony going? _____

2. What is the fine for? _____

B.

As soon as they arrived, Meg headed straight for the new exhibit. The enclosure had obviously been redesigned. It is much larger and even has an area labeled "Primate Playground."

1. Where is Meg and has she ever been there before? _____

2. What is she viewing? _____

C.

Tom had always hoped he would someday be able to visit the states. Now, with his father's announcement, his dream would come true. They would be flying directly from London to "The Big Apple." "At least we speak the same language," he thought.

1. What was Dad's announcement? _____

2. In what country does Tom live? _____

Directions: Read the sentence, then determine the meaning of the idiom from the list below. Write your answers on the lines provided.

1. The coach told the team to **get the lead out**.

   _____

2. Mom jogs every day and is **as fit as a fiddle**.

   _____

3. After the fall, the skater didn't know **which way was up**.

   _____

4. The news reporter said that the stock market **took a dive**.

   _____

5. Every time Grandma sees me, she says I've **grown like a weed**.

   _____

6. The real estate salesperson said she had some **hot property**.

   _____

7. Marga really got herself **in a pickle** this time.

   _____

8. The movie had me **rolling in stitches**.

   _____

- stuck in a jar
- in good physical condition
- jumped into a pool
- on fire
- move faster
- laughing hard
- plays an instrument
- was confused; disoriented

- take out their pencils
- decreased significantly
- in a difficult position; in trouble
- valuable; for sale at a good deal
- needing surgical repair
- gotten taller quickly
- misjudged direction
- appear messy and out of place

Here's a tool you can use to help you better understand what you read: compare and contrast. That just means alike and different.

Directions: Think about the two things paired below. Write one way they are alike (compare) and one way they are different (contrast).

1. **lion tiger**

Alike: _____

Different: _____

2. **sled skis**

Alike: _____

Different: _____

3. **sun moon**

Alike: _____

Different: _____

4. **job career**

Alike: _____

Different: _____

5. **dragon unicorn**

Alike: _____

Different: _____

6. **vitamins minerals**

Alike: _____

Different: _____

7. **arctic antarctic**

Alike: _____

Different: _____

Directions: Read about two famous people and match them to the statements below. Write Edison, Einstein, both or neither in the spaces provided.

Thomas Edison

Thomas Edison lived from 1847 to 1931. This American is considered by many the greatest inventor of all time. With only three months of formal schooling, Edison was able to patent more than 1,100 inventions. He experimented in many fields and even predicted the use of atomic energy. Among his incredible achievements, he is credited with changing the world forever by giving it the electric light. He also invented one of the first successful motion picture devices, worked on the development of sound movies, and invented the phonograph, paving the way for the movies and music we enjoy today.

Edison viewed his work not as genius but as tireless effort. He defined genius as "1 percent inspiration and 99 percent perspiration."

Albert Einstein

Albert Einstein, a native of Germany but later an American citizen, lived from 1879 to 1955. He is considered one of the greatest scientists of all time. He attended public school and then went on to study mathematics and physics at the Polytechnic Institute in Zurich, Switzerland. After graduating in 1900, Einstein worked on several concepts as yet unknown to science. He is best known by the public for his theory of relativity and his equation $E=mc2$, which became the cornerstone of the development of atomic energy. This, and his other achievements, revolutionized the world's concepts of time, space, and matter.

When it was suggested that only a handful of people could understand and test his theory, Einstein insisted that anyone with a good grasp of higher mathematics could do so.

_____ 1. Was alive and working in 1900

_____ 2. Paved the way for today's entertainment industry

_____ 3. Was born an American citizen

_____ 4. Is considered among the greatest in his field

_____ 5. Viewed his work as beyond the capabilities of others

_____ 6. Had a passion for understanding how things work

_____ 7. Had many years of formal schooling

_____ 8. Had thought about atomic energy before it was a reality

_____ 9. Is directly responsible for major change in the world

_____ 10. Was mainly concerned with global scientific theory

_____ 11. Invented things that profoundly affected how everyday people live

Directions: Read about making lists of the world's wonders. Then follow the directions below.

"World's Greatest"

Dating back to early civilizations, people have enjoyed making lists of the "world's greatest." This is evidenced by what we know today as "The Seven Wonders of the Ancient World." This list was actually just one of several the ancient Greeks compiled of the marvelous structures known to them at the time. Like any "world's greatest" list, it is subjective. It contained such human-made things as The Great Pyramids of Egypt and The Hanging Gardens of Babylon.

Another list of "world's greatests" is that of "The Seven Wonders of the Natural World." Of course, this list can include only things created by nature, such as the Grand Canyon, the Giant Sequoia Forest, or Mount Everest.

Today, travelers and explorers are still fond of making "world's greatest" lists, such as "The Seven Wonders of the Modern World," on which the Golden Gate Bridge or the Eiffel Tower might appear.

In reality, a "world's greatest" list could consist of almost any category or number of things that are superlative to the creator of the list. It's a personal judgment. What would you include in your own list of "The Seven Wonders of the World"?

1. To make sure you understand the the passage, define the following words as they're used:

subjective: _____

superlative: _____

2. Do a little digging (in an encyclopedia or on the Internet) to find lists of "The Seven Wonders of the Ancient World", and of the "Natural World." Compare and contrast them.

_____

_____

_____

_____

3. Answer the question posed at the end of the passage: What would you include on your own list of "The Seven Wonders of the World"? _____

_____

_____

_____

Directions: List the similarities and differences of a frog and toad. You may want to refer to an encyclopedia or the Internet for more information.

- Spends most of its adult life in water
- Has a long, sticky tongue
- Goes through a tadpole stage
- Has smooth, moist skin
- Moves in short hops
- Is classified as an amphibian

- Has dry, bumpy skin
- Feeds mainly on insects
- Begins life as an egg in water
- Moves in long leaps
- Spends most of its adult life on land
- Has a stocky, compact body

SIMILARITIES

FROG

_____

_____

_____

_____

_____

_____

_____

_____

DIFFERENCES

TOAD

_____

_____

_____

_____

_____

_____

_____

_____

_____

_____

Based on your answers, do frogs and toads have more similarities or differences? _____

Similes, metaphors, and idioms are expressions that mean something other than what they say.

Directions: Similes and metaphors are figures of speech used to make a description more lively. For example, a phrase such as "I was hungry" could become "I was as hungry as a bear," or "My stomach was roaring." Learn more about them below.

> A **simile** is a comparison using *like* or *as* (You are as cool as a cucumber).
> A **metaphor** compares one thing directly to another (You are the cream of the crop).

A. Choose and write a **simile** to replace each sentence.

1. It was loud. _____

2. It looked shiny. _____

3. It moved fast. _____

4. It was cold. _____

5. It was old. _____

B. Choose and write a **metaphor** to replace each sentence.

1. I was scared. _____

2. "Go now!" he yelled. _____

3. It moved slowly. _____

4. It was raining hard. _____

5. The car was no good. _____

- barked out
- crawled along
- as quick as lightning
- a lemon
- like a refrigerator

- as hot as fire
- sparkled like diamonds
- a real chicken
- flew
- like a snail

- boomed like thunder
- as old as the hills
- like rose petals
- drop me a line
- buckets

NAME _____   DATE _____

Directions: Each sentence contains an idiom. Underline it. Then write the intended meaning.

An idiom is a an expression that, if taken literally, would make little or no sense. The words mean something entirely different from what they say (That's the way the cookie crumbles).

1. You'll get a kick out of idioms. _____

2. Jarred flew home from school. _____

3. It was raining cats and dogs. _____

4. Lorraine has a green thumb. _____

5. Please lend me a hand. _____

6. I had to eat my words. _____

7. Look at it with an open mind. _____

8. Tonight I have to hit the books. _____

9. You can't pull the wool over my eyes. _____

10. Mom put her foot down on that idea. _____

11. Traffic was heavy today. _____

12. We have to straighten up the house. _____

13. We were just hanging out. _____

Choose three idioms from above and draw what they would mean if taken literally. Have fun!

#____	#____	#____

Directions: The story below contains similes, metaphors, and idioms. Find and identify them.

Homer and Horace

When I asked mom if I could have a pet snake, she said I had rocks in my head and suggested hamsters instead. Ok, so hamsters aren't exactly as cool as snakes, but they have their merit. At least they DO something, instead of just sitting like a bump on a log. I agreed.

At the pet store, the salesperson warned me that, although hamsters are cute, you have to watch them like a hawk. Apparently, they are master artists of escape. She sold me a sturdy cage, some toys, and two hamsters that looked as innocent as babies.

So, back at home, I kept an eye on Homer and Horace. All they did was scamper around, play, and eat. Days went by. And there was no attempt to escape. I began to think the girl at the pet store was pulling my leg. More days went by. Then weeks. My little prisoners stayed put.

Then, one day, after I had put my fears to rest, I checked the cage. You could have knocked me over with a feather! No, they were there all right, but something was in there with them. Under the shavings I heard a rustling—quiet—but as clear as day. Babies!

The next day I went into the pet store. She was there—that mountain of information about hamsters. I caught her attention. Just as I was about to blast her for warning me about the wrong thing, she cheerily asked how Homer and Horace were doing. Suddenly my anger floated away. "They're great," I said, "but I've had to change Horace's name to Doris."

"Oh," she said, her face turning as red as a beet, "I forgot to give you the OTHER warning about hamsters."

Similes: (comparisons using like or as) _____

_____

_____

Metaphors: (direct comparisons) _____

_____

Idioms: (non-literal expressions) _____

_____

_____

_____

_____

How good are you at spotting exaggeration—stretching the truth to make a story more exciting? You've probably done it a million times!

Directions: Exaggeration is one of the hallmarks of the type of folklore known as tall tales. In fact, the term tall tale is sometimes used to mean exaggerated. Below are some excerpts from tall tales. Underline any examples of exaggeration.

A. from "Paul Bunyan"

When Paul was a baby, he rolled out of his cradle and mowed down a mile of trees. And he snored. No, no ordinary snore. When Paul snored it was louder than a thunderstorm. By the time he was a teenager, Paul was fifty feet taller than the other boys. It was hard to find friends. Then one day he saw a blue mountain, only it wasn't a mountain. It was a mountain-size blue ox named Babe.

B. from "John Henry"

John Henry could swing a hammer faster than lightning. And he was so strong he could drive a railroad spike with one blow. Sometimes he worked so fast that sparks flew from his hammers. John, in fact, used two hammers at once and each weighed over twenty pounds. One time someone had to pour water on his hammers to keep them from catching fire while he worked.

C. from "Pecos Bill"

Pecos Bill could invent anything, so some people asked him to invent a way to make it rain. Bill took his lasso, which was really a snake thirty feet long, and caught a cyclone he spotted over Oklahoma. He squeezed the rain out, then rode it all the way to California. He hit the ground so hard that it made a valley. That's where Death Valley came from, and it is still there today.

Directions: An author may use exaggeration, not expecting it to be believed exactly as stated, but to liven up a story or make a point. Below you will have a chance to recognize exaggeration when you see it and make up some of your own.

A. *Choose the underlying meaning of each exaggeration.*

1. I could do that with my hands tied behind my back.

    O I am strong enough to lift that alone.   O I think the task is easy for me.

2. It was taller than a house and wider than a barn.

    O It was unusually large.   O It had a huge square shape.

3. My room looked like a tornado had hit it.

    O It was messy.   O It was soggy and wet from rain.

4. It will take a month of Sundays to finish this math homework.

    O The homework is hard.   O It will take a long time to do it.

B. *Complete the answer to each question with an exaggeration.*

1. *How hungry was he?* He was so hungry that _____

    _____

2. *How hot was it?* It was hot enough to _____

    _____

3. *How deep was it?* It was deep enough to _____

    _____

4. *How pretty was it?* It was prettier than _____

    _____

5. *How fast was it?* It was so fast that _____

    _____

6. *How old was it?* It was older than _____

    _____

As you read for information, look for two things: specific facts about the topic and generalizations. Remember: A generalization must be valid for everything it refers to.

Directions: As you read this passage, think about what general statements could be made about the subject covered. Then follow the two-part directions below.

Seeing Stars

A constellation is a grouping of stars that, to ancient peoples, suggested the form of a picture. Constellations such as Orion, Leo, and Pegasus are named after characters in Greek mythology. Orion was a fearless hunter, Leo, a mighty lion, and Pegasus, a winged horse. The Greeks named 48 constellations in all. Many others followed.

Each constellation appears within a definite region of the sky. Ancient travelers used their knowledge of the positions of constellations to help them navigate. It is possible, even today, to locate stars, planets, and other stellar objects by their relative positions to the constellations.

Though it takes a stretch of the imagination to see images such as Orion the hunter, Leo the lion, or Pegasus the flying horse, these ancient sky pictures have survived for thousands of years.

A. *Is the statement a generalization or a specific detail? Write **G** or **S**.*

_____ 1. Constellations appear in a particular region of the sky.

_____ 2. Orion, Leo, and Pegasus are constellations.

_____ 3. The position of constellations can be used for navigation.

_____ 4. A constellation is a grouping of specific stars.

_____ 5. The ancient Greeks recognized and named 48 of the constellations.

_____ 6. Constellations are named for a particular image suggested by the arrangement of stars.

B. *Write a sentence of your own. Make it a generalization about the duration of the Greek's version of the constellations they recognized and named.*

_____

_____

Directions: Following the passage below are several generalizations about the subject. Some are valid, some are not. To be a valid generalization, the statement must be true in all cases. Write VALID or INVALID before each statement.

Medal of Honor

Perhaps you have read and enjoyed books such as *Caddie Woodlawn, Island of the Blue Dolphins,* and *A Wrinkle in Time*. These, and others you may recognize, are among a select group of children's books to receive the prestigious honor known as the Newbery Medal.

The Newbery Medal is an award given to honor the most distinguished children's literature book published in the previous year by an American author. It was first awarded in 1922.

The award was established by Frederic Melcher, who at the time was chairman of the board of the publishers of the *Library Journal* and *Publisher's Weekly*. Melcher named the award after John Newbery, an 18th century English publisher and bookseller who is credited with being the first person to put children's literature in print. In addition to the Newbery Medal, Melcher also founded its counterpart for illustration, the Caldecott Medal. Today the Newbery Medal is awarded by the Children's Services Division of the American Library Association.

_____ 1. The Newbery Medal is a prestigious award.

_____ 2. To receive the Newbery award, the book must have been published in the previous year.

_____ 3. Only American authors are considered for the Newbery award.

_____ 4. Everyone agrees that each winner is deserving.

_____ 5. Only authors of children's books can receive medals of honor.

_____ 6. The Newbery Medal has been awarded yearly for more than 80 years.

_____ 7. John Newbery lived and died well before the award was created.

_____ 8. Today, the Newbery Medal continues to be awarded each year to one outstanding author of a children's book.

_____ 9. Only one outstanding children's book is published each year.

CHALLENGER: It is technically possible for one person to receive both the Newbery and the Caldecott Medal. How could that be? _____

Directions: Read the following passage. In each set of sentences below, circle the sentence that is a valid generalization.

Norway

Norway is a long, narrow country on the northwestern side of Europe. About one-third of the country lies inside the Arctic Circle. This northern area is sometimes called The Land of the Midnight Sun because in the summer months, the sun never sets completely and there is daylight 24 hours a day.

Norway can be divided into four land regions. One is the Highlands, which are characterized by rocky peaks and glaciers. This area runs along the east side of the country. Next are two areas of lowlands. The Southeastern Lowlands has rolling countryside and land suitable for commercial and industrial use. It is in this area that Oslo, the capital is located. The other lowland area is known as the Trondheim Lowlands. This area consists of many wide, flat valleys, making it especially good for farmland. The final region is the Coast and Islands. More than 150,000 islands lie off the Norwegian coastline, which itself is about 1,650 miles long. The rocky coastline is characterized by many inlets, called fiords.

The latitude of Norway lends itself to some very frigid weather. While this is certainly the case inland, along the coastline, the sea tempers the weather. In fact, along the west coast, the winter in Norway can be warmer than the winter in Chicago, which is much farther south. It is easy to see why many Norwegians live along the coastal areas.

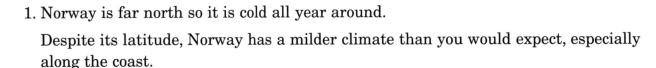

1. Norway is far north so it is cold all year around.

   Despite its latitude, Norway has a milder climate than you would expect, especially along the coast.

2. In summer north of the Arctic Circle, there can be daylight 24 hours a day.

   Half of Norway is known as the Land of the Midnight Sun.

3. Norway's lands consist of mountains, rolling hills, flat valleys, and rocky coastline.

   Many Norwegians live along the coast because it is warmer.

4. Norway is always warmer than Chicago.

   Though further north, the west coast of Norway can be warmer than Chicago in winter.

5. Norway is a country on the northwest coast of the continent of Europe.

   Norway's capital is Olso, which lies in the Trondheim Lowlands.

Summarizing helps you recognize the point of what you are reading.

Directions: Summarizing is a useful note taking tool when reading for information. First, scan the passage for key words. Second, identify the main topic or subject. Finally, read the entire passage and jot down a few short sentences that restate the key ideas.

A. *Use the paragraph to practice the three steps to summarizing.*

If you have ever walked along a rocky shoreline or a pier, you probably noticed a crusty looking coating on the rocks or wood of the pilings. That "crust" is actually a congregation of animals called barnacles. A barnacle is a small shellfish that, when it reaches adulthood, permanently attaches itself to some surface. The only thing that moves for the rest of its life are its feathery tentacles, which it uses to draw in food. Once attached, barnacles are practically impossible to remove. They have been a nuisance to seamen since there have been ships. A crust of barnacles can slow a ship down and affect its steering and machinery.

STEP 1: While scanning the paragraph, what key words did you spot? _____

_____

STEP 2: What is the main topic or subject? _____

STEP 3: Restate the key ideas in two or three short sentences. *(TIP: Reread each sentence. Evaluate if it gives key information or is a detail not essential to learn and remember about the topic.)*

_____

_____

_____

_____

B. *Apply these steps to a passage in one of your textbooks or an informational article in an encyclopedia or other resource. First write out the steps as outlined above. Then fill in the answers for your selection.*

Directions: Use the Summary Example as a guide to write a summary of the two stories listed below. Then write one of your own choice.

Summary Example

You have no doubt read summaries in movie and TV listings, reviews, and other sources. Take a look at this tongue-in-cheek summary of "The Three Little Pigs". What elements does it include? What does it purposely leave out?

> **"The Three Little Pigs"** Three brothers try to avoid being lunch for a wolf. Undaunted, the wolf manages to seemingly trap them together in a house. Just as he is about to succeed, the pigs lure him into a trap.

"Cinderella" _____

_____

_____

_____

_____

"The Wizard of Oz" _____

_____

_____

_____

_____

" _____ **"** _____

_____

_____

_____

_____

Directions: Janice read an article and wrote a summary about opinion polls. Evaluate her summary by answering the questions. Then rewrite it so that it is improved.

Opinion Polls

(1) An opinion poll is a way of finding out what many people think by asking a few. (2) Several methods are used. (3) These are personal interviews, phone interviews, and written questionnaires. (4) Reliability of results depends on many factors, but the most important are the size of the sample group and whether the sample group is random. (5) A random sample is a group that represents people of all different types in the population. (6) Opinion polls are used for politics, business, and research.

1. What key words are important in Janice's summary?

_____

2. What sentence number is the topic sentence? _____

3. Could sentence #2 and #3 be combined? _____

4. Could sentence #4 be shortened? _____

5. Is sentence #5 needed? _____

Use the answers from your evaluation to write an improved version of Janice's summary:

_____

_____

_____

_____

_____

_____

_____

CHALLENGER: Work with a partner. Choose an article that interests you both to summarize. Write your summaries separately, then trade to compare and evaluate. Finally, put both of your best ideas together to write one, improved version.

A movie preview gives you a good idea of what is to come and gets you ready for the story. Previewing what you read can do the same thing.

Directions: A movie preview lets you predict what kind of movie it is, such as comedy or action. Previewing what you read can help you identify what kind of writing it is. We classify literature by genre (zhän rə), which simply means type. Use the clues in the writing previews to predict the genre of each excerpt.

Realistic Fiction

Biography

Fantasy

Historical Fiction

Folklore

Mystery

Science Fiction

Poetry

1. ...There, near the mouth of the cave, he could feel the hot air—the breath of the dragon! It must be in there!...

_____

2. ...One of the books looked odd—yes, it was fake. The insides were designed to hide something valuable. But what?...

_____

3. ...If I were a lion, tall and proud.
My roar would be low and loud....

_____

4. ...The young Union soldier looked up briefly, his eyes focused on just one Confederate approaching. It was his cousin, William!

_____

5. ... Harvey Firestone grew up on a farm in Ohio. He became interested in rubber tires while working for a carriage factory...

_____

6. ...Peter could not believe his ears. "Mom," he protested, "do I really have to take my dumb little brother along?"

_____

7. ...The landscape was not as they had expected. It was red. If it weren't for the two glowing moons, they'd have lost the ship...

_____

8. ... John Chapman traveled west, spreading appleseeds everywhere he went. Folks got to calling him Johnny Appleseed...

_____

Directions: One reason to preview what you read is to determine its point of view. Read the explanations below. Then identify from which point of view each passage was written.

first person
The focus is on the *writer*. Uses words such as I, me, us, and we.

second person
The focus is on the *reader*. Uses words like you and your.

third person
The focus is on the *subject*. Uses words such as it, they, them, he, she, and names.

1. If you want to earn a little extra money, consider pet-sitting. Before you take on a job, however, be sure you know the owner and you spend a little time with the pet to make sure you can handle the job.

   This is written in the _____ person.

2. When I want a treat that is yummy and good for me, too, I whip up one of my favorite things—a banana yogurt shake. I just plop a banana in the blender with some plain yogurt, and tah dah, it's done.

   This is written in the _____ person.

3. While at the L.A. Zoo, you will want to be sure to see the koala exhibit. You won't find the koalas outside, though. You'll find them housed in a darkened building that simulates night, which is when koalas are most active.

   This is written in the _____ person.

4. The fir tree is shaped like a triangle. It belongs to the evergreen group of trees. It has cylinder-shaped cones and its needles are its leaves. Fir trees can be very pleasantly fragrant.

   This is written in the _____ person.

5. In southern Florida there is a large area of wetlands called the Everglades. It is rich in wildlife and supports such unusual creatures as alligators, manatees, and the Florida panther.

   This is written in the _____ person.

6. Write a short paragraph containing the word *encroached* in a third person point of view.

   _____

   _____

   _____

Directions: Recognizing point of view is an important previewing skill. Review the meanings of first, second, and third person. Then go on a search for real-life examples in books and stories.

first person

The focus is on the *writer*. Uses words such as I, me, us, and we.

Find an example of a piece of writing done in the first person. Identify the source, then copy two sentences from it: _____

_____

_____

second person

The focus is on the *reader*. Uses words like you and your.

Find an example of a piece of writing done in the second person. Identify the source, then copy two sentences from it: _____

_____

_____

third person

The focus is on the *subject*. Uses words such as it, they, them, he, she, and names.

Find an example of a piece of writing done in the third person. Identify the source, then copy two sentences from it: _____

_____

_____

NAME _____ DATE _____

Directions: Before reading, skim the passage for any unfamiliar terms. Jot them down. Then go back and read the sentences containing unfamiliar words. If you still can't predict the meaning use a glossary or dictionary to look it up. Then, read the whole passage.

Ken wanted to know about the Constitution. He looked it up in the encyclopedia. Part of what he found is here. Ken picked out three unfamiliar terms. He predicted what he thought they might mean. Decide if you agree or disagree with his predictions, write your own, then look up the meaning of the words. Finally, evaluate your prediction.

A constitution is the basic set of rules that governs a country. The constitution of a country usually provides for the form of government, for limits on the government's powers, and for assurances of the rights and **liberties** of the citizens. In order to make the rules of the constitution lasting, the process of **amending** the constitution has been made difficult. For example, to amend the United States Constitution, both the Senate and the House of Representatives must **ratify** the amendment by a two-thirds vote. Amendments can also be ratified by a three-fourths vote of the states. If a court finds that a law passed by Congress conflicts with the Constitution, the law is declared unconstitutional, and cannot be enforced.

1. Ken thinks **liberties** means *laws*. ☐ I agree with Ken ☐ I disagree with Ken

   I think it means _____.

   The dictionary says liberties means_____.

   Who was right? (check one) ☐ Ken ☐ Me ☐ Both ☐ Neither

2. Ken thinks **amending** means *changing*. ☐ I agree with Ken ☐ I disagree with Ken

   I think it means _____.

   The dictionary says amending means_____.

   Who was right? (check one) ☐ Ken ☐ Me ☐ Both ☐ Neither

3. Ken thinks **ratify** means *vote*. ☐ I agree with Ken ☐ I disagree with Ken

   I think it means _____.

   The dictionary says ratify means_____.

   Who was right? (check one) ☐ Ken ☐ Me ☐ Both ☐ Neither

NAME _____   DATE _____

Directions: Have you ever come across a foreign phrase while reading and lose your train of thought? Previewing can help avoid that. Here are some common foreign terms to learn now, so you'll be ready for them next time. Then, choose the phrase that belongs in the sentence.

à la carte: according to the menu   **au contraire**: on the contrary

au revoir: until we meet again   **bona fide**: in good faith

carte blanche: with full authority   **eureka**: I have found it

hors d'oeuvre: appetizer   **laissez faire**: noninterference

modus operandi: manner of working   **protege**: under the guidance of another

non sequitur: does not follow   **status quo**: as is; the way things are

vice versa: conversely; in reverse   **voilà**: there it is

1. She believed his apology was _____.

   O *bona fide*   O *au contraire*

2. They bid each other _____ and parted.

   O *à la carte*   O *au revoir*

3. He was a _____ of the karate master.

   O *protege*   O *carte blanche*

4. The police knew the criminal's _____.

   O *hors d'oeuvre*   O *modus operandi*

5. The government's policy was _____.

   O *laissez faire*   O *voilà*

6. She stared at him and _____.

   O *eureka*   O *vice versa*

7. Let's keep the arrangement _____.

   O *status quo*   O *non sequitur*

Mapping is a great way to organize and remember information. And, it's not only useful, it's fun!

Directions: Mapping is showing information in a visual way. Read the story below, then write short sentences or phrases to complete the story elements map.

The day began like most others did here on the prairie in the summer of 1847. It was hot and dusty. My throat was as dry as a bone and our horses were looking ragged. After bumping along for hours in the afternoon sun, someone in a wagon up ahead said they spotted a creek. A drink and a splash in the water sure sounded refreshing at this point. The caravan slowed and came to a stop. We all got buckets out to fill at the stream and bring back to the horses.

Just as we were making our way toward the sound of gurgling water, the horses started to buck and whinny. I looked at Dad and saw fear in his eyes. Something was spooking the horses. If we strained our ears we could make out the sound of hoofs coming closer. I took a deep breath and squeezed my eyes tight. No one moved. The sound got louder and louder until I knew they were right upon us. Then suddenly it stopped. Afraid to look, but having to know, I opened my eyes. There they were—several men on horses—waving at us! It seems someone from their caravan had seen ours stop, and sent scouts over to see if we were OK.

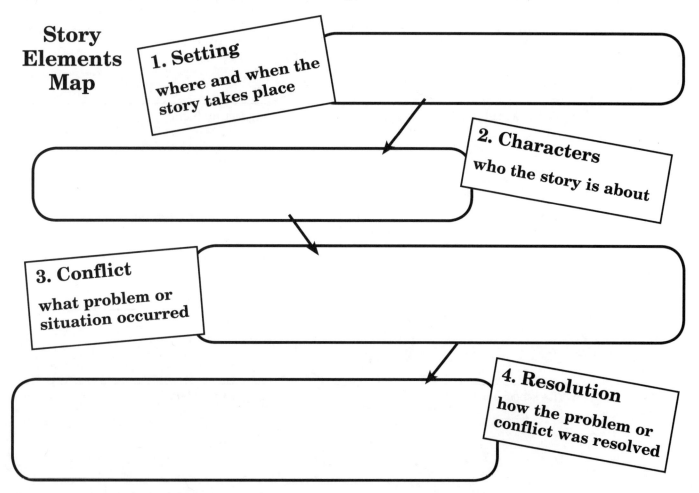

Story Elements Map

1. Setting where and when the story takes place

2. Characters who the story is about

3. Conflict what problem or situation occurred

4. Resolution how the problem or conflict was resolved

NAME _____   DATE _____

Directions: Read the paragraphs about Dan and Don. Then fill in the character maps for each.

Dan

Dan is an eighth-grade boy. He lives in Atlanta, Georgia. He likes reading and sports, especially baseball. He has an older brother and a younger sister. Dan says his best trait is honesty. He says his biggest problem is saving money. When he grows up he hopes to be a sports agent.

Don

Don lives in Seattle, Washington, where he is in the eighth grade. His favorite subject in school is math, but he also enjoys playing soccer. He has a younger brother and no sisters. Don says his best trait is reliability. He says his biggest problem is being tall. When he grows up he wants to be a teacher.

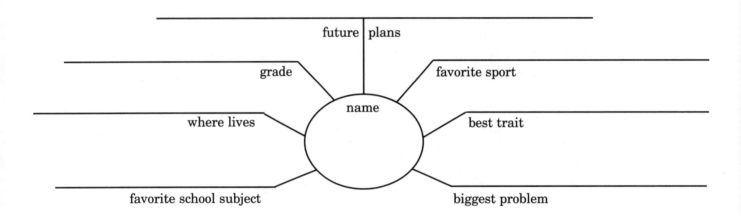

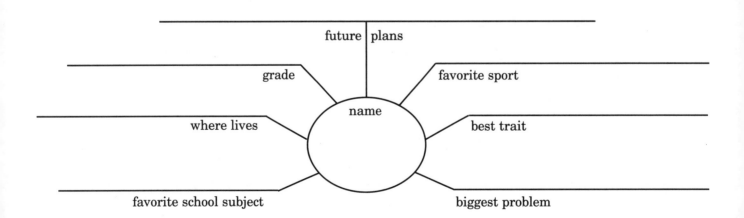

Directions: Making a map is a fun way to analyze and compare characters. Imagine that you and a friend are characters in a story. Fill in the first character wheel about yourself and the other about your friend.

Directions: First find each listed character trait in the word search puzzle. Then below, pick a character from a story you've read. Fill in four character traits that apply to that character. Use words from the list or your own. Add a sketch of his or her likeness.

spirited	G	C	S	D	M	O	K	C	I	F	E	A	H	B	O	G	E	C	L	A

spirited
sly
smart
mysterious
devious
clever
honest
shy
tough
cautious
nervous
impatient
brave
selfish
skeptical
mean
funny
faithful
sweet
cheerful
proud
wicked
polite
friendly
witty

G C S D M O K C I F E A H B O G E C L A
M I B L Y P O D T S L M P R O U D B S H
R A E N S W I C K E D H C B E S I J M C
C T W I T T Y G C L M D A I C W L E A U
H O J B E L R A I F O B G D U E B R R S
E E C I R M F N F I M P A T I E N T T B
E D E V I O U S D S P F W C S T E O A D
R B T U O I N L K H B A A Y I C R F E G
F R O F U D N S P I R I T E D N V A M O
U M U R S L Y H F C J T N S H Y O I E B
L S G I B E B A B A F H E A D H U C A K
A L H E A C R I O E P F A C I O S M N A
K Y E N D C A U T I O U S K G N T B R C
F B A D F P V B A C S L O C L E V E R S
D I G L S K E P T I C A L M C S O N A E
O C L Y B H E C F D G P O L I T E H F B

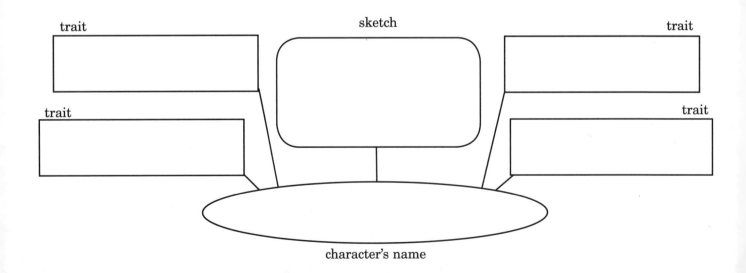

trait

trait

sketch

trait

trait

character's name

Common Core Skills & Strategies for Reading: Level 8

Directions: One way an author gets you "into" a story is by telling you how a character feels as the story unfolds. Read the story below. Complete the map that follows the character's feelings.

It's Only Natural

The last thing Keith wanted to do was go to the Museum of Natural History. In his mind museum plus history equaled boring. Besides, some of the guys had asked him to go to the park to roller blade that Saturday. But, no, it was "family day" and the museum it was.

Keith lagged behind even his little brother as they walked from the parking lot to the entrance. He caught up at the ticket line. As he had his hand stamped, he glanced around the main hall. He expected to see stuff like old pictures of people he didn't know or care about and rusty relics of machines that were used for things that didn't even exist anymore. Instead, in the center of the big hall was a full-scale model of a mastodon, his long tusks curling upward and trunk extending several feet out.

Several archways led to other halls. Keith read the signs—and realized that he had jumped to conclusions. History, especially, natural history, might be quite interesting.

Keith does not want to go to the Museum because he wants _____
_____

Keith goes to the museum anyway because
_____
_____

Keith assumes he won't like the museum because he thinks _____
_____
_____

In the parking lot, Keith lags behind because
_____
_____

When Keith sees the mastodon he feels _____
_____

At the end, Keith feels _____
because he didn't understand what natural history was and had jumped to conclusions. He decides
_____
_____

Directions: The characters may be interesting, but it's the plot that hooks us into reading a story. The plot is the progression of events in the story. Read the retelling of the fable, "The Dog and His Bone." Then complete the map of its progression of events.

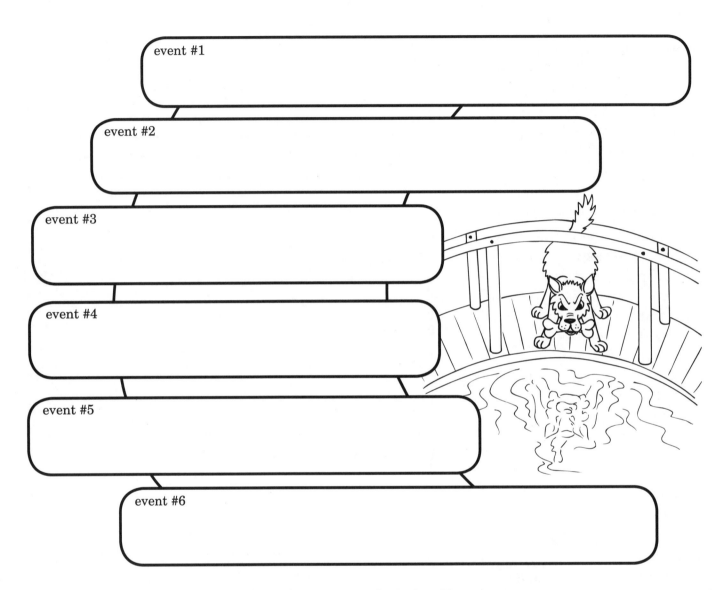

event #1

event #2

event #3

event #4

event #5

event #6

The Dog and His Bone

A frisky dog was bounding along with a juicy bone he had found. His thoughts were on how much he would enjoy gnawing the bone on the front porch at home. On the way, he had to cross a wooden bridge over a stream with water that reflected like a mirror. As he crossed, he was stunned to see a dog, just like him, with another nice, juicy-looking bone. At once, he decided he must have that bone, too. His plan was to scare the other dog off, then grab the bone. He leaned over to face the dog in the water and barked his scariest bark. In doing so, he dropped his own fine bone into the water, where it sank immediately. The hound walked home not with two bones, but none.

Moral: Greed can make one act foolishly.

Directions: The elements of a fiction story are setting, character(s), problem or conflict, and resolution (how the problem or conflict is solved). Complete the story map below for a book you have recently read or one you remember well.

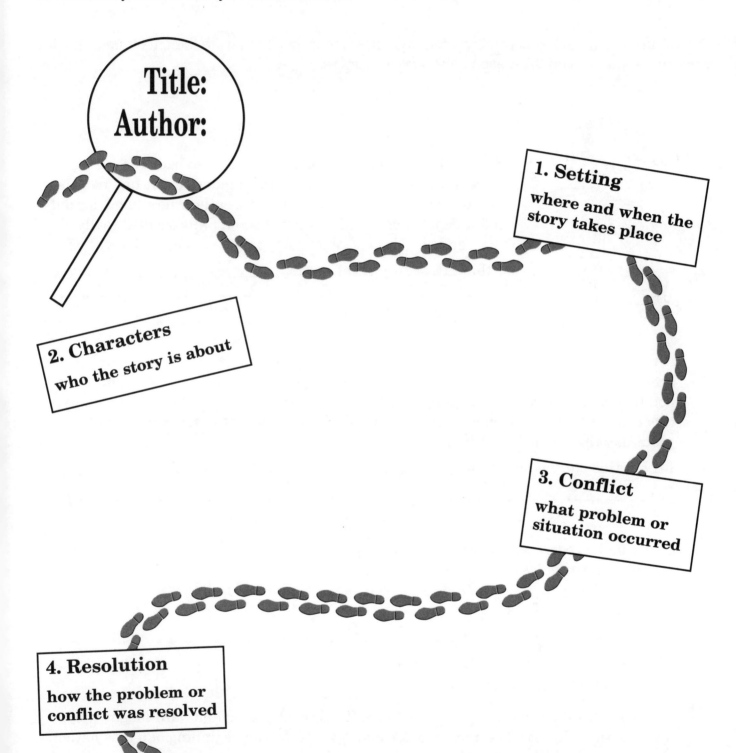

Title:
Author:

1. Setting
where and when the story takes place

2. Characters
who the story is about

3. Conflict
what problem or situation occurred

4. Resolution
how the problem or conflict was resolved

In a story you can travel through time—past, present, or future. Before you begin to read, set the time frame by scanning for a time reference.

Directions: Read each excerpt. Look for time reference clues. Then write the time frame—past, present, or future—and the reason behind your decision.

A. Abby decided living in a log cabin wasn't so bad. True, it wasn't as comfortable as her old home in England, but it had its good points. For one, they'd been settled into their new home for only a few days when she met a new friend. Sally seemed really nice, and she showed Abby how to make a doll from cornhusks.

I think this story is set in the _____ because _____ _____.

B. Steve knew months must have passed, but he had no concept of how long. When the pod lid opened, he thought only about taking that first breath. Had he really been in this capsule while the computer took them to a distant planet? It seemed like only yesterday that he had gone into stasis.

I think this story is set in the _____ because _____ _____.

C. Jenna had a report coming up and as she logged on to the Internet, she smiled. She was remembering last year when she had to do that report on weather, and they weren't online yet. It sure would have been easier. Compared to last year's report, this should be a piece of cake.

I think this story is set in the _____ because _____ _____.

D. The men all sat around the great oak table. It had been a long and hard-fought war, but now the colonies were free. This document would be the beginning of a new nation. Thomas dipped his pen into the inkwell, ready to sign.

I think this story is set in the _____ because _____ _____.

Directions: Test your ability to place events in proper time sequence. Read the story and the statements that follow it. Decide if each would have happened before or after the events in the story. Write BEFORE or AFTER.

It's Cookie Time

Mrs. Jackson is in the kitchen. "I'd better get going," she says to herself, thinking of the call from John just a few minutes ago. "It's time. I'll be bringing Benny and the girls over." Mrs. Jackson smiles and wrinkles her nose.

Mrs. Jackson is a widow now but still lives in the big old house where she raised her whole family. She remembers baking cookies for Carl and JoAnn and their smiling faces after following the scent home from school. Carl lives in Michigan with two boys of his own now, but JoAnn, John, and their three children still live just down the way. And, this Saturday morning, she is making a batch of those cookies for them—enough to last the whole weekend while JoAnn is in the hospital having her fourth child.

_____ 1. Mrs. Jackson bakes cookies for her children.

_____ 2. Mr. and Mrs. Jackson live in the big old house.

_____ 3. JoAnn goes to the hospital.

_____ 4. Mrs. Jackson's grandchildren come to visit.

_____ 5. Carl moves to Michigan.

_____ 6. JoAnn has her third child.

_____ 7. JoAnn's husband, John, calls Mrs. Jackson.

_____ 8. Mrs. Jackson becomes a grandmother.

_____ 9. JoAnn has her fourth child.

_____ 10. Carl eats Mrs. Jackson's cookies.

_____ 11. JoAnn picks up the scent of the cookies.

_____ 12. Mrs. Jackson watches three of her grandchildren.

_____ 13. Mrs. Jackson has six grandchildren.

_____ 14. Benny is born.

You have different moods, and so do stories. The author chooses certain words to set the tone of the story and to guide you into the right mood for reading it.

Directions: Read each excerpt. Choose the mood you think the author is trying to convey. Then underline or highlight the words that set the tone.

1. The sun had gone down, leaving us with only the light of the moon to find our way. We knew we were on the right path but were not sure how far it was back to camp. The path was dim and I could hear things rustling in the grass near my feet as I walked. The trees seemed to grow taller, and their branches became like arms reaching for us.

   O eerie   O lonely   O tender

2. Shifting yet again in his seat, Ray glanced once more at the clock. He rolled his eyes, let out a sigh, and picked up a magazine. He turned the pages quickly, not even noticing that it was the same magazine he had looked through five minutes ago. He had never had a tooth pulled before and just wanted to get it over with.

   O humble   O nervous   O bored

3. "Late! Again! And on test day!" Brianna thought as she jumped out of bed. In fifteen minutes flat she went from sleeping to entering the classroom. "What a break," she said to herself. The teacher had her back to the class, and she could slip in quietly, maybe even unnoticed. As Brianna slid into her seat, the silence became muffled laughter. The teacher turned and followed everyone's eyes to Brianna, where she sat still wearing her pajama pants—the ones with the pink teddy bears!

   O thrilling   O magical   O comical

4. Matt and Gary had been best friends since the first grade. As Gary looked around his room, everything seemed to remind him of Matt—his baseball glove (they had spent a lot of hours tossing the ball), his Battleship game ("I sunk your aircraft carrier!"), and the pictures (especially the one of them together smiling, both without front teeth). Mom called Gary for dinner, but he just sat on his bed. "What am I going to do without Matt?" he said almost out loud.

   O serious   O cautious   O suspenseful

Common Core Skills & Strategies for Reading: Level 8

Directions: Compare the moods of the two poems below. Then answer the questions.

Sound Awake

I'm all tucked in, I've cleared my head,
And even though I'm in my bed,
I cannot go to sleep.

I fluff my pillow and turn it 'round,
I'm hearing every little sound.
I cannot get to sleep.

I scratch an itch on my knee.
I check the clock–it's after three!
I cannot get to sleep.

I count the stripes on the wall.
It doesn't do a thing at all.
I cannot get to sleep.

I've been lying here half the night.
Could it be it's getting light?
And *now* I'm g o i n g t o s l...

Fast Asleep

I hear my bed beckoning
It waits so soft and comfortably
I stretch, I yawn,
I crawl inside...
The sheets are clean and fragrant
My blanket like a feather covers me
My pillow snuggles 'round my head
And I sink into its softness.
A cool breeze kisses my face.
My eyes grow heavy.
And in a moment
I'm resting on a cloud
Being carried away
Drifting, Drifting...
D r i f t i n g
a
  s
   l
    e
     e
      p

1. Compare the two poems. Write "same" or "different" for each description:

   a) subject _____ b) mood _____ c) form _____

2. Compare the titles of the two poems. How do they set the tone for what is to come?

   _____

3. The first poem has rhyme and rhythm. The author almost makes the words tick like

   a clock. How does this fit the subject of the poem? _____

   _____ Why do you think the second poem has no

   rhyme or rhythm? _____

4. What technique did both authors use to emphasize the action of falling asleep? _____

   _____

5. Think of two words to describe the mood of each poem: Sound Awake: _____

   _____ Fast Asleep: _____

A worm looks different to you than it does to a bird. Your perception of something changes depending on your point of view. This is true for stories too.

Directions: Below are excerpts from different stories. Decide if the story is being told by the author as if from personal experience, told by a fictional character in the story, or told by an outside narrator.

1. ...Suddenly she looked at the clock and saw that it was a quarter to twelve. Remembering the Fairy Godmother's warning, she dashed for the golden coach...

   _____

2. ...I saw the box with my own eyes. It really did exist. At first, I couldn't find the courage to look inside. Then I thought of the captain's words...

   _____

3. ...Bah, humbug. I don't see why all this merriment is necessary. It seems to me like just an excuse to take a day off from work...

   _____

4. ...His request seemed reasonable. It was the least I could do after he scared the hunter away and probably saved my life. So I bent down low, where he could crawl up onto my antlers, and I carried him across the rushing stream...

   _____

5. ...It had been a hard climb. The wind was biting cold, and sometimes we could barely see through the swirling snow. Yet, we felt confident we would make it to the top. That was until Jefferson slipped. His ankle swelled inside his boot and he couldn't walk...

   _____

6. ..."Has the mail come yet?" Michael asked. "On the table," answered Mom. "Are you..." But before she could finish, Michael had already found what he wanted and was out the door with it. He opened the envelope gingerly. He knew this letter could change his life...

   _____

Directions: The story below is written from a narrator's point of view. Rewrite the first part from the spider's point of view. Rewrite the second part from the fly's point of view.

A. It was morning in the garden on a lovely spring day. Spider got up early. He had a lot of work to do. He was moving today. First, he looked around the garden, assessing which spot would be best for catching meals. When he settled on the space between the wheelbarrow and the wall, he got his eight legs moving. For hours he spun and shaped his new web. By noon it was done and he was hungry. He hoped a nice juicy fly would happen by.

_____

_____

_____

_____

_____

_____

_____

B. Fly was enjoying the lovely spring day in the garden. In the morning he was out looking for something for breakfast. He buzzed around the flowers a while but then caught the scent of something sweet. Strawberries! He landed on a ripe one, had his fill, and was ready for a nap. He took off toward the wheelbarrow. He was sleepy but not sleepy enough to notice that the coast was no longer clear. Had the sun not been shining he might not have noticed that Spider had a new home.

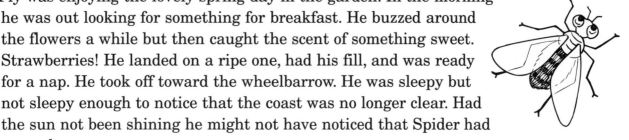

_____

_____

_____

_____

_____

_____

Directions: Imagine that a reporter is interviewing three characters from the classic story *Peter Rabbit*. Answer the questions as you think each character would.

MR. McGREGOR

Q. How did you feel when you found Peter's jacket in your garden?

A. _____

Q. Everybody has to eat. Why are you so adamant about not sharing with your rabbit neighbors?

_____

_____

Q. What are you planning to do to prevent future raids on your garden?

A. _____

_____

PETER RABBIT

Q. What made you disobey your mother's orders and go into Mr. McGregor's garden?

A. _____

Q. What was your first thought when you realized Mr. McGregor spotted you?

_____

Q. Looking back, do you think it was foolish or courageous to go into the garden, and why?

A. _____

Q. If you had it to do all over again, what would you do differently?

A. _____

_____

MRS. RABBIT

Q. Some are saying that your punishment of Peter was too severe. How do you justify it?

A. _____

Q. Do you think Peter has learned a lesson, or will you have to watch him more closely, and why?

_____

_____

Directions: Read the story about Jessica and her younger sister, Lisa. Answer the questions.

The Campout

Jessica looked out her window and saw the glow of the lantern inside the tent in the back-yard. Her younger sister and her friends decided it would be cool to "camp out." Jessica rolled her eyes. She was fourteen and had been on real camp-outs. "Fifth graders," she mumbled. "Kids."

Jessica picked up a book from her desk. Before plopping down on her bed to read, she cracked the window open a little. "Just in case," she thought, "so I'll hear if there's trouble."

She did hear quite a lot, but it wasn't trouble. The three girls were giggling and having a great time. Jessica tried to concentrate on her book but found herself back at the window. A foot with a fuzzy pink slipper hung out the flap of the tent. There was a jar of fireflies in the grass. Jessica glanced at the clock. 10:23. "Shouldn't those kids be settling down by now?" she thought.

At 10:27, Jessica heard nothing. She didn't bother to look out the window. She just went downstairs and out into the back yard. The tent was dark, but she still heard hushed voices inside. She opened the flap and stuck her head in. All three girls screamed and got tangled up in their sleeping bags trying to huddle together. Then they realized it was Jessica. "You guys OK?"

"We were reading a scary story when our lantern burned out, so we decided to go to sleep. Then YOU showed up and REALLY scared us. You probably did it on pur-pose, too!" Lisa snapped.

She didn't, of course, but she also didn't mind having done it.

1. How does Jessica feel about fifth graders and why? _____

_____

2. How does the author let you know that Jessica cares about her younger sister? _____

_____

3. Underline any of the following words you think apply to Jessica in this story:

   envious   protective   meddlesome   nosy   responsible   stuck-up   nervous

4. How do you think Lisa would characterize her big sister? _____

5. If she heard nothing, why did Jessica go outside to the tent? _____

_____

6. If Jessica did not purposely scare the girls, why did she not mind that she did? _____

_____

Authors have a purpose in mind when they write. It may be to describe, inform, instruct, persuade, summarize, or entertain.

Directions: Learn more about these purposes for writing in Parts A and B below.

A. Match each purpose for writing on the left to its explanation on the right.

describe · · · · · · · · · · · to give directions; tell how to

instruct · · · · · · · · · to convince

inform · · · · · · · · to paint a visual picture

persuade · · · · · · · · to express creatively

summarize · · · · · · · · to share facts or information

entertain · · · · · · · · to explain in short

B. Fill in the correct purpose for each example of writing.

1. The main purpose of an **advertisement** is to _____ the reader to buy something.

2. The main purpose of a **movie review** is to _____ the story for the reader.

3. The main purpose of a **recipe** is to _____ the reader how to prepare a dish.

4. The main purpose of a **notice** is to _____ the reader about events, times, and dates.

5. The main purpose of a **brochure** is to _____ the features of a place.

6. The main purpose of a **cartoon** is to _____ the reader with creative humor.

Directions: Read each paragraph topic below. Write the probable purpose for writing the paragraph: *to describe*, *to instruct*, *to inform*, *to persuade*, *to summarize*, or *to entertain*.

Topic 1

installing your new software

purpose:
_____

Topic 2

my best birthday ever

purpose:
_____

Topic 3

why you should eat a good breakfast

purpose:
_____

Topic 4

the beauty of fall in New England

purpose:
_____

Topic 5

what to pack for summer camp

purpose:
_____

Topic 6

how to make your own bookcase

purpose:
_____

Topic 7

highlights of my trip to Alaska

purpose:
_____

Topic 8

sights and sounds of the circus

purpose:
_____

Topic 9

wearing seatbelts can save your life

purpose:
_____

NAME _____   DATE _____

Directions: When you read, look for clues to the writer's purpose. Is the writing meant to describe, instruct, inform, persuade, summarize, or entertain? The puzzle below will help you.

The answers to the clues fit in the puzzle, one letter to a blank. To solve the puzzle, write the correct answers on the lines. Then read the word under the ★. Use it to answer the question below.

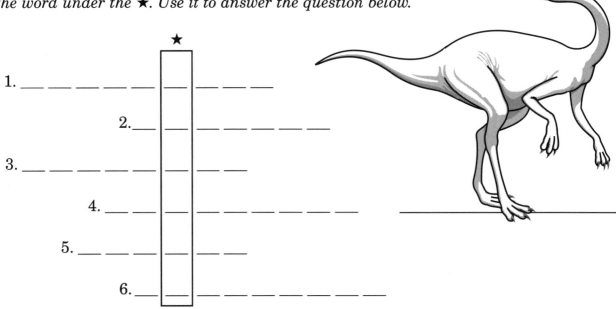

★

1. __ __ __ __ __ __ __ __ __

2. __ __ __ __ __ __ __ __

3. __ __ __ __ __ __

4. __ __ __ __ __ __ __ __

5. __ __ __ __ __

6. __ __ __ __ __ __ __ __ __

Question: What does all writing have?   **Answer:** a _____ !

1. Most likely to contain **generalizations**: writing meant to _____

   Ex: *Many scientists now agree that several dinosaurs were more like birds than reptiles.*

2. Most likely to contain **many sensory adjectives**: writing meant to _____

   Ex: *I was famished so I had honey ham, crisp lettuce, juicy tomato, and sweet pickle on whole wheat.*

3. Most likely to contain **strong opinions**: writing meant to _____

   Ex: *Everyone should have a cell phone. They're great for emergencies or just chatting.*

4. Most likely to contain **step-by-step directions**: writing meant to _____

   Ex: *First, gather your materials. Next, cut the top off the milk carton...*

5. Most likely to contain **factual details**: writing meant to _____

   Ex: *The wingspan of the brown bat is about 13 inches. The tail is less than half of the body length.*

6. Most likely to contain **characters** and/or **plot**: writing meant to _____

   Ex: *When the giant walked across the channel, tidal waves hit the shore.*

Pull all your reading skills together and test your total comprehension.

Directions: Read the story about geysers and answer the questions.

A Natural Wonder

Geysers are among the most fascinating and unusual phenomena in the geologic world. These amazing eruptions can shoot boiling hot water and steam hundreds of feet in the air. Though found on every continent except Antarctica, geysers are rare. It is estimated that there are less than 700 in all. Incredibly, Yellowstone National Park has more than half of all the world's known geysers!

Just what is a geyser? The U.S. Geological Survey defines it as "a hot spring characterized by intermittent discharge of water ejected turbulently and accomplished by a vapor phase." For a geyser to occur, the conditions must be just right. First, there must be a plentiful, permanent source of water on the surface. This can come from rain and snow. Second, there must be a volcanic heat source below the surface. Third, the surrounding rock must be of a certain type—that which can produce a material called geyserite. Finally, the springs and channels that carry the water up must be of a special shape, including a narrow opening at the surface. With all these exact conditions necessary for a geyser to form, no wonder they are so rare.

1. What was the author's purpose: describe, inform, or entertain? _____

2. What word in the story means *more than one phenomenon*? _____

3. Underline the best estimate of the number of geysers in Yellowstone: 75   600   1   350

4. If you previewed the passage, you made a prediction about the meaning of the word *intermittent*. What did you think it means? _____

   What is its dictionary definition? _____

5. How many special conditions must be met for geysers to occur? _____

6. Name one way a geyser is like a volcano, and one way it is different. _____

   _____

7. Reread the official definition of a geyser. Now define it in your own words. _____

   _____

8. Is this passage science fiction, nonfiction, or realistic fiction? _____

Directions: Read the story, then check your comprehension by answering the questions.

Choosing a Pet

There are lots of things to take into account when you are considering getting a pet dog or cat. First, your pet will need more than a home. It will need daily attention in the form of food, water, and love. But, that's just the beginning. You will need to provide a comfortable place to sleep, space and toys for play, and attend to its grooming needs. Your pet should see a vet for health check-ups and regular immunizations. You will need to monitor your pet for signs of sickness or injury and ensure that its environment is conducive to its safety.

Other responsibilities will vary depending on the kind of pet you get. Dogs, in general, have lots of energy and need opportunities to run around. Large dogs especially should not be confined to small areas. At the minimum a dog needs to be walked frequently (and cleaned up after). A dog also needs human stimulation and interaction. You must be willing to commit to spending time with your dog. This means time playing, but also time teaching and training.

Though still dependent on you for its basic needs, a cat requires less direct attention. If you provide and regularly clean a litter box, a cat can happily spend its whole life indoors. A cat also will take care of its own grooming needs. Cats spend a lot of time sleeping or napping and probably the most attention they will want from you is to play occasionally or to sit on your lap and be petted.

So how do you choose? Dogs are high-maintenance but can give a lot back in terms of emotion and interaction. Cats are lower maintenance, but also less responsive to you. If you want a loyal friend, a dog is the better choice. If you prefer an acquaintance, then perhaps a cat is for you.

1. Is this passage written in first, second, or third person? _____

2. What word in the story means *watch over time*? _____

3. Compare and contrast dogs and cats in terms of time commitment. _____

_____

_____

4. If you previewed the passage, you made a prediction about the meaning of the word

   conducive. What did you think it meant? _____

   What is its dictionary definition? _____

5. Which sentence in paragraph two is an opinion? _____ A generalization? _____

6. What word in the story is a synonym for *shots*? _____

7. What is the root word of *responsive*? _____

8. Complete this sentence with *its* or *it's*: _____ your job to provide for _____ needs.

9. Is this passage science fiction, non-fiction, or realistic fiction? _____

NAME _____ DATE _____

Directions: Read this story then answer the questions.

One Tough Tortoise

My dad and I belong to ARC, the Arizona Reptile Club. Once a month we ge[t] reptile lovers (yes, you can love a reptile) to swap information and stories. One the club organized a trip to the desert. It was supposed to be like a safari—we wo[u] try to spot reptiles in their natural habitat, then report back what we saw at the nex[t]

So, off we went—reptile lovers armed with cameras. After driving for a while, we were o[n] road through open desert. We were moving slowly looking for signs of life. That's when I saw sized tortoise who had made his way just about across the road. Suddenly a large pick-up truck up on our tail, honking. The driver was waving his fist and yelling. We pulled over a little to the si[de] and he stepped on the gas to pass us, leaving a cloud of smoky dust behind. When the cloud settled, I glanced back at the tortoise. He was not at the side of the road where he had been a moment ago. I leaped from the car and crossed the road where I scanned the area like a hawk. About 20 feet out, I saw him—or at least I saw a shell—turned over on its back. It had to be him and that truck must have clipped him as it passed and sent him hurling.

One of our goals as an organization is to preserve and protect wildlife, so we were furious at the prospect of having one of our beloved creatures assaulted in his own domain. Dad joined me and we sadly walked over to where he lay, unmoving. "It doesn't look good, Marsha," he said as he bent down and turned the shell upright.

I stood there just staring at the shell, tears starting to well up. Then something amazing happened. A little head gingerly poked out, then the legs. In a moment, the tortoise had lifted himself up on his toes. He looked back at us once, as if to say thanks, then walked away.

"That's one tough tortoise," said Dad.

"Yep," I said smiling and took a picture of "Mr. T."

1. Is the storyteller a boy or a girl? _____ How can you tell? _____

2. Is the story written in first, second, or third person? _____

3. Find a simile in the story. _____

4. Which of the following can you conclude is a character trait of the storyteller?
   O devious   O compassionate   O dependent   O hot-tempered

5. By reading the first sentence, what can you infer about how the storyteller thinks most people feel about reptiles? _____

6. Write a synonym for: a) glanced _____ b) swap _____

7. In this story clipped means: 1. cut away, 2. joined together, or 3. hit on the edge?

   _____

8. Is the figure of speech *armed with cameras* a simile, metaphor, or idiom? _____

DATE _____

A mile is a mile. Or is it? Read this story to find out. Then answer the questions.

How Far is it?

is a unit of length. But how far is it? That depends on when and where you are.

ile was first used by the Romans and defined as 1,000 paces of five
or roughly 5,000 feet. In fact, the term mile comes from the Latin
ds milia passuum, meaning a thousand paces. Technically, if you were
a Roman of short stature, your mile would be shorter than that of
your taller neighbor.

Around 1500, the mile was changed to 5,280 feet. Why? Because
in the 1500s Englishmen measured distances in 660-foot furlongs,
so the Queen made the mile 8 furlongs. The United States adopted
this mile and it remains the standard length
today—unless you live in a country that has a different definition or
that measures in the metric system. In the latter case, a kilometer is
3,280.8 feet, or approximately 5/8 of a mile.

The mile we have been talking about so far applies to distance on
land, sometimes referred to as land mile or statute mile. On sea or
in the air, a mile is something else—precisely 1/60 of a degree of the distance around the
earth. Therefore an air mile or nautical mile is 6,076.1 feet. The international nautical mile
is equal to 1.1508 statute miles. A knot is a measurement of speed. If a ship covers one
nautical mile per hour, its speed is one knot.

Now you have it all straight, right? As straight as a Roman mile!

_____

1. What was the author's purpose: summarize, inform, or persuade? _____

2. If you walked a half mile, how many furlongs is that? _____ How many feet? _____

3. If a car went one mile per hour and a ship one knot, which covers more distance? _____

4. What language was used by the Romans? _____

5. Which distance is shorter: a kilometer or a land mile? _____

6. In paragraph 3, what does *the latter* refer to? _____

7. What term used in the story refers to the ocean or sea? _____

8. What word in the story is a synonym for *height*? _____

9. Find a simile in the story: _____

10. What is the difference between an air mile and a land mile? _____

11. What is the current length of a statute mile in the U.S.? _____

12. Give two meanings of the word *knot*: _____, _____

13. What is your opinion of this story and why? _____

_____

To use a dictionary, glossary, thesaurus, encyclopedia, or index, need to have excellent alphabetizing skills.

Directions: Practice alphabetizing to the third letter of the following words.

A. Match each word on the left to its meaning on the right. Write its letter on the line.

____ 1. **undaunted**   A. not afraid; not discouraged

____ 2. **legible**   B. firm; steadfast; not giving in

____ 3. **unyielding**   C. free time

____ 4. **leisure**   D. escort; bring in

____ 5. **unique**   E. one of a kind

____ 6. **irrigate**   F. supply with water

____ 7. **unscrupulous**   G. without regard for rights

____ 8. **usable**   H. easy to read; plain and clear

____ 9. **irksome**   I. fit for use

____ 10. **usher**   J. tedious; tiresome; annoying

B. To solve the puzzle, write the words above in alphabetical order, one letter to a blank. Read the word under the ★. Fill it in above the meaning on the note. Then use it in a sentence.

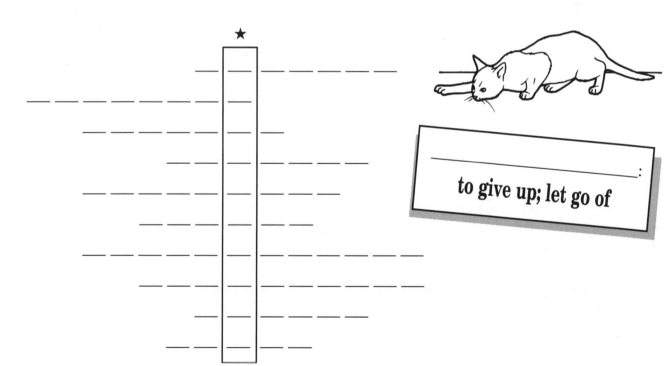

to give up; let go of

Directions: Alphabetizing is fairly straightforward until you get to titles, authors, and illustrators. Study the rules for alphabetizing titles and names, then write the lists in alphabetical order.

A. WHEN ALPHABETIZING TITLES:
Do not count words such as The, An, and A at the beginning of a title.

B. WHEN ALPHABETIZING NAMES,
Use the last name and list it first, followed by a comma and the first name

A Visit to William Blake's Inn	Maurice Sendak
Winnie-the-Pooh	Beverly Cleary
The Jungle Book	Louisa May Alcott
A Christmas Carol	Paul Goble
An Apple for Miss Jones	Laura Ingalls Wilder
The Cat in the Hat	Jean C. George
Jumanji	Chris van Allsburg
A Wrinkle in Time	E. L. Konigsburg
Arrow to the Sun	Janice May Udry
One Fine Day	E. B. White

1. __An Apple for Miss Jones__

2. _____

3. _____

4. _____

5. _____

6. _____

7. _____

8. _____

9. _____

10. _____

1. __Alcott, Louisa May__

2. _____

3. _____

4. _____

5. _____

6. _____

7. _____

8. _____

9. _____

10. _____

A dictionary lists thousands of words alphabetically. But how can you quickly find the word you're looking for? There are guide words at the top of each page that identify the first and last word on the page.

Directions: Imagine that you want to look up the words below in a dictionary. You have opened to the pages shown below. Look at the guide words. Then for each word below, decide if it would be on one of these pages, before these pages, or after these pages. Write BEFORE, AFTER, or the page number.

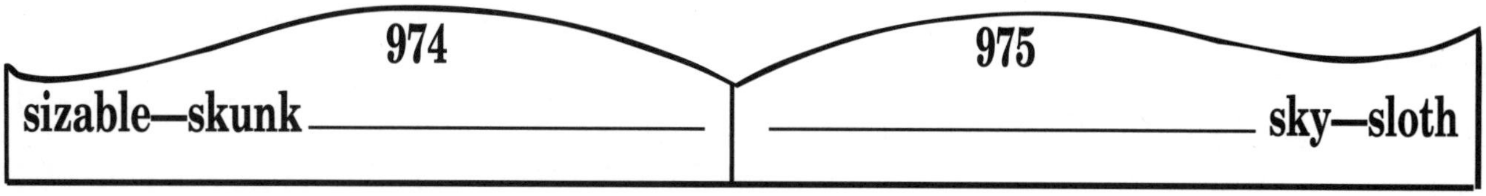

974	975
sizable—skunk	sky—sloth

_____ 1. slab

_____ 2. slough

_____ 3. sizzle

_____ 4. snag

_____ 5. slag

_____ 6. simulate

_____ 7. sloppy

_____ 8. skew

_____ 9. sole

_____ 10. slime

_____ 11. smear

_____ 12. skimp

_____ 13. siphon

_____ 14. slant

_____ 15. slur

_____ 16. skeptic

_____ 17. shrill

_____ 18. sledge

_____ 19. snicker

_____ 20. shrewd

Directions: You use a dictionary to look up word meanings and spellings, but there is another feature that can really help you with reading: the dictionary tells you how to pronounce words. Let's see if you can use this tool. On each note below is the pronunciation of a word from the dictionary. Write the word it represents.

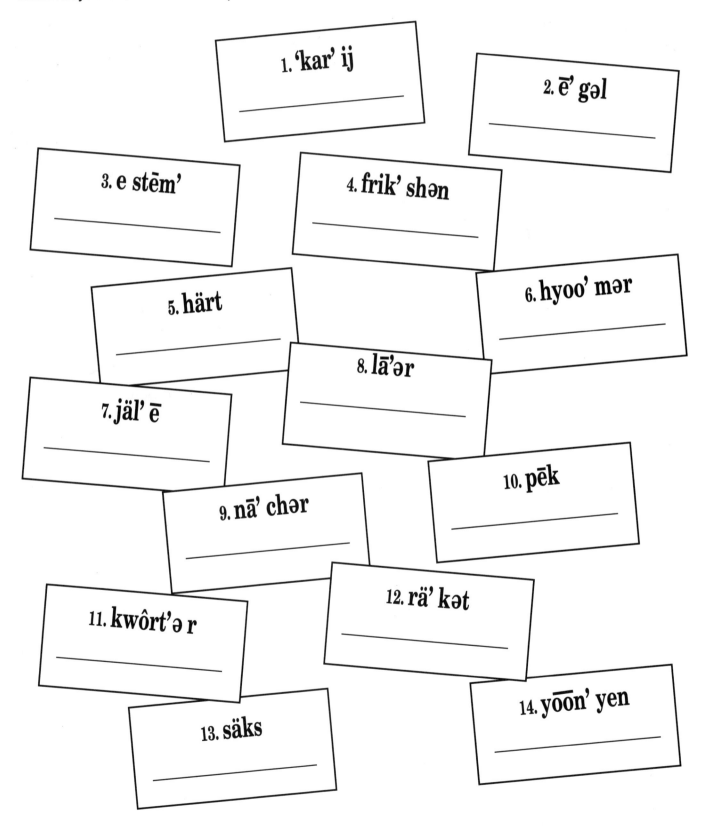

1. ‘kar’ ij
_____

2. ē’ gəl
_____

3. e stēm’
_____

4. frik’ shən
_____

5. härt
_____

6. hyoo’ mər
_____

7. jäl’ ē
_____

8. lā’ər
_____

9. nā’ chər
_____

10. pēk
_____

11. kwôrt’ə r
_____

12. rä’ kət
_____

13. säks
_____

14. yoon’ yen
_____

NAME _____ DATE _____

Directions: Use a dictionary to find the answers to the questions below. You may work alone or team up with a partner.

1. What is a **capybara**? _____

_____

2. How is the word **cuisine** pronounced? (Write the pronunciation)_____

3. Which meaning of **legend** would relate to maps? (Write the number and meaning)

_____

4. What is the origin of the word **pet**? _____

5. What does the title **Ph.D**. stand for? _____

6. What does the Latin phrase *caveat emptor* mean? _____

7. Where is **Easter Island**? _____

8. Where would you be able to see a **quoin**? _____

9. What does an **insomniac** have trouble doing? _____

10. What is a synonym for **procure**? _____

11. What would an Irishman do with an **ulster**? _____

12. Does the first syllable of **cayenne** rhyme with *sky* or *ray*? _____

13. A **jota** is a Spanish dance. How is it pronounced? _____

14. What shape is a **tondo**? _____

15. On what syllable is the accent in the word **salubrious**? _____

16. From what language do we get the word **tovarish**? _____

17. What is the first sound in the word **phlox**? _____

18. Would it be a good idea to **mollify** a crying baby? _____

Now answer these question about your search.

The dictionary I used was _____

I was able to find the answers to _____ of the 18 questions.

The most interesting thing I came across was _____

Something that surprised me was _____

Something new I learned about using a dictionary is _____

Many textbooks offer a glossary to help readers with new terms.

Directions: Study the two excerpts from textbook glossaries below. Then read each statement. Decide if it applies to Glossary A, Glossary B, Both, or Neither.

A. **Acute Angle** An angle that has a measurement less than 90°.

Addend A number that is added. In 6 + 3 = 9, the addends are 6 and 3.

Area A number indicating the size of the inside of a plane. The area of this figure is 6 square units.

Associative Property of Addition A rule that states that the way in which addends are grouped does not affect the sum. (2 + 4) + 3 = 2 + (4 + 3)

B. **adaptation** (ad ap tā' sh ə n) A body part or activity that helps a living thing to survive. p. 129

air pressure The downward push of the air in the atmosphere. p. 186

algae A group of non-seed plants that do not have true roots, stems, or leaves. p. 232

anemometer (an ə mom' ət ə r) An instrument used to measure wind speed. p. 188

_____ 1. lists terms that may be unfamiliar to the reader

_____ 2. provides pronunciation for some terms

_____ 3. includes definitions of all words used in the book

_____ 4. gives the origin of the word defined

_____ 5. includes a picture or diagram for clarification

_____ 6. presents words in alphabetical order

_____ 7. gives the page number where it is introduced

_____ 8. is specific to the subjects covered in the text

_____ 9. would be found in a science textbook

CHALLENGER: How is a glossary like a dictionary? How is it different? _____

_____

_____

_____

Looking for something particular in a book? Check the table of contents. You'll find it at the beginning of the book.

Directions: Use the table of contents below to answer the questions.

Table of Contents

1. In what chapter would you find information about volcanic rock? _____

2. What pages offer definitions of the main types of rocks? _____

3. Do these chapters cover how gold is formed? _____

4. On what page are rubies and emeralds compared? _____

5. Where can you find out how gems are priced? _____

6. Does this book cover decorative gems? _____

7. On what page would you find out about erosion? _____

8. Where can you find out how crystals are formed? _____

9. Where could you find out the difference between a gem and a common rock? _____

10. The book covers building with what three rocks? _____

_____

Start with the index at the back of a book when you are searching for specific information.

Directions: Look at the excerpt of an index below. Use it to answer the questions.

1. Based on the index, what do you think is the subject of this book? _____

2. How is an index organized? _____

3. Where could you find out about tarantulas? _____

4. What kinds of animals are found in the section of this book between pages 84 and 85? _____

5. Is there information about sand dollars in this book? _____

6. You looked for information about whale sharks under *W* and found nothing. Where else might you find it? _____

7. Look at the animals listed for pages 103 and 104. What do they have in common that suggests this book is arranged by type of animal? _____
_____

8. On what page do you think seals are mentioned but not thoroughly discussed? _____ Why? _____
_____
_____

9. A sidewinder is a specific type of what animal? _____
   (Hint: look at the page number)

10. What type of animal do you think a siamang is and why? _____
_____
_____

When you think of reading, you may only think of books and stories. But you also read graphs, tables, diagrams, and maps.

Directions: A timeline is one type of graphic that helps you visualize events over time. Below is a timeline of some notable U.S. lunar missions. Use it to answer the questions.

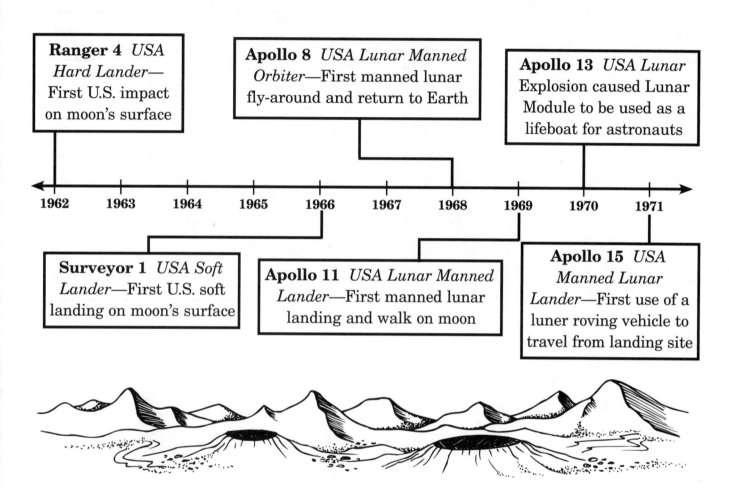

1. What years does this timeline span? _____

2. On what mission was the first American soft landing on the moon? _____

3. When was the first U.S. manned orbit of the moon? _____

4. On what mission did a man first set foot on the moon? _____

5. In what year was the first contact with the moon made by a U.S. craft? _____

6. On what mission was a lunar roving vehicle put into service? _____

7. Why didn't Apollo 13 make a lunar landing? _____

_____

NAME _____ DATE _____

Directions: Graphs are a way of presenting information so you can easily see and compare data. Below are two graphs of the same data. Use them to answer the questions.

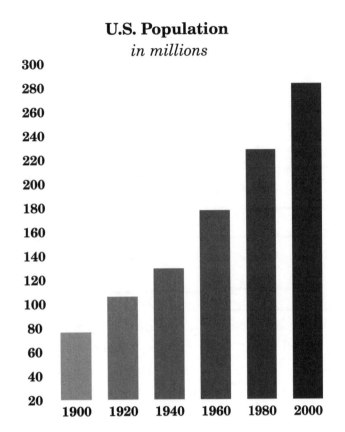

1. What does the number 100 stand for on the left of each graph? _____

2. How many people does each line on graph 2 represent? _____

3. For what century does each graph track population? _____

4. For what 10-year period was growth the slowest? _____

5. About what year did the population reach 200 million: 1961, 1970, 1979? _____

6. Does the bar graph or the line graph give more precise information? _____

7. On which graph is it easier to see rate of growth? _____

8. On which graph is it easier to see relative amounts? _____

9. If you were born in 1980, about how much has the population increased since you were born? _____

Directions: A diagram is another way to present information visually. Study the diagram below, then answer the questions.

Life-Supporting Cycles
Oxygen, Carbon Dioxide, Water

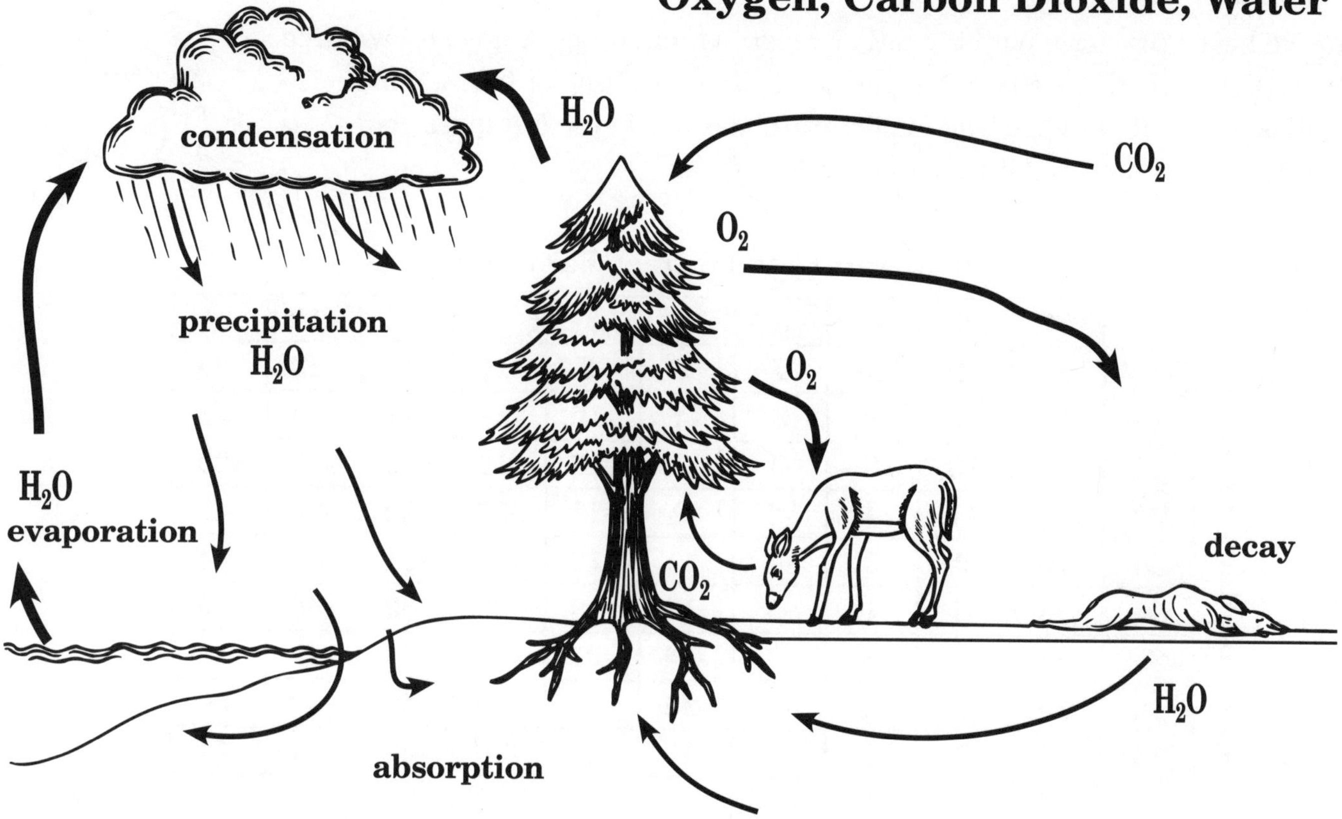

1. What is the chemical symbol for oxygen? _____ carbon dioxide? _____ water? _____

2. Which word on the diagram means *rain or snow*? _____

3. What do animals exhale when they breathe? _____

4. What word on the diagram means *to drink up*? _____

5. Do plants absorb or give off carbon dioxide? _____

6. When an animal decays, what is absorbed in the soil? _____

7. When water evaporates does it rise or fall? _____

8. What element, needed by animals to breathe, do plants give off? _____

9. What would happen if one of the three cycles was interrupted? _____

_____

Directions: A table is a way of presenting information in an organized, easy-to-read way. Use this table to answer the questions.

Wind Chill

You've heard this term on the weather report—if not describing your own area, then that of another's whose temperatures dip to freezing or below. Wind chill is the combination of the temperature and wind speed. It gives you an idea, not of how cold it is, but how cold it *feels*.

Temperature in Degrees Fahrenheit

	30	25	20	15	10	5	0	-5	-10	-15
5	25	19	13	7	1	-5	-11	-16	-22	-28
10	21	15	9	3	-4	-10	-16	-22	-28	-35
15	19	13	6	0	-7	-13	-19	-26	-32	-39
20	17	11	4	-2	-9	-15	-22	-29	-35	-42
25	16	9	3	-4	-11	-17	-24	-31	-37	-44
30	15	8	1	-5	-12	-19	-26	-33	-39	-46
35	14	7	0	-7	-14	-21	-27	-34	-41	-48
40	13	6	-1	-8	-15	-22	-29	-36	-43	-50
45	12	5	-2	-9	-16	-23	-30	-37	-44	-51
50	12	4	-3	-10	-17	-24	-31	-38	-45	-52
55	11	4	-3	-11	-18	-25	-32	-39	-46	-54

Wind Speed in Miles Per Hour

1. When it is 0° with a wind speed of 15 mph, how cold does it feel? _____

2. Would it feel colder at 10° with 5 mph wind or 20° with 35 mph wind? _____

3. Other than at 0° with no wind, when could it feel like 0°? _____

4. What is the warmest temperature it can be and still feel like below 0°? _____

5. How much difference does a 10 mph wind make on a 0° day? _____

6. If the temperature is 30° and the wind is 30 mph, how cold does it feel? _____

7. Would you rather be out on a day that is 15° with 45 mph wind or a day that is 5° with a 5 mph wind? _____

8. What is the lowest temperature you think you have ever been outdoors in? _____

NAME _____   DATE _____

Directions: At some point, you will undoubtedly be called upon to read a map. Refresh your map-reading skills by imagining you are visiting downtown Pinewood.

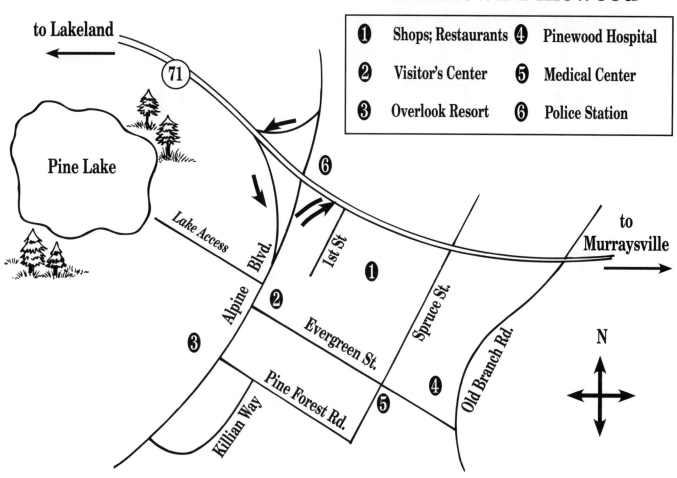

Downtown Pinewood

❶ Shops; Restaurants   ❹ Pinewood Hospital

❷ Visitor's Center   ❺ Medical Center

❸ Overlook Resort   ❻ Police Station

1. In what direction from Pinewood is Pine Lake? _____

2. What is at the intersection of Evergreen St. and Old Branch Rd.? _____

3. What main highway runs through Pinewood? _____

4. In what direction is the Medical Center from the Shopping District? _____

5. You are at the Visitor's Center, where you find out there is a homemade candy shop on Killian Way, near Pine Forest. How do you get there? _____

_____

6. Can you get on Rte. 71 from Spruce St.? _____

You are at the Overlook Resort. How do you get from the resort on to Rte. 71 east?

_____

NAME _____   DATE _____

Do you skip reading the directions or instructions? If so, you are probably missing important information that will help you succeed.

Directions: Below is a made-up test information sheet. Follow the directions carefully to fill it out. Pretend that your student ID number is 307295.

SECTION 1

A.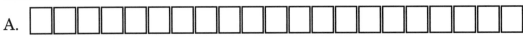

B.

C. ☐   D. ☐☐   E. ☐☐ ☐☐ ☐☐

SECTION 2

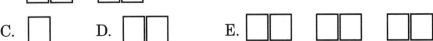

0	0	0	0	0	0
1	1	1	1	1	1
2	2	2	2	2	2
3	3	3	3	3	3
4	4	4	4	4	4
5	5	5	5	5	5
6	6	6	6	6	6
7	7	7	7	7	7
8	8	8	8	8	8
9	9	9	9	9	9

SECTION 3

① ② ③ ④

SECTION 4

⓪ ① ② ③ ④ ⑤

INSTRUCTIONS

Section 1, Part A: Fill in your name, last name first, one letter to a block. Use all capitals. Leave a space between your last and first name.

Section 1, Part B: Fill in your date of birth, starting with month, then day, then year. Use 2-digit numbers (February = 02).

Section 1, Part C: Fill in your gender. M or F

Section 1, Part D: Fill in your grade.

Section 1, Part E: Fill in today's date, starting with month, then day, then year. Use only two-digit numbers (February = 02).

Section 2: Write your student ID number on the blanks. Then fill in each number in the column below. Fill in the circle completely.

Section 3: Fill in the circle that represents which quarter of the year you are taking this test: Sept.-Nov.–1; Dec.-Feb.–2; March-May–3; June–Aug.–4.

Section 4: This is for office use. Leave it blank.

NAME _____ DATE _____

Directions: Not following instructions (or trying to skip them entirely) can cause problems, and, in some cases, be dangerous. Darryl was trying to install a CD player in his computer. Read the instructions below. Then answer the questions.

Installation Instructions

Step 1: Have these materials handy: Phillips screwdriver, pair of pliers, installation guide, CD drive, and software installation disk.

Step 2: Before attempting to install anything, turn off your computer and unplug it!

Step 3: To gain access to the inside of the computer, remove the cover carefully. If this is the first time you are doing this, consult your computer's instruction manual.

Step 4: To avoid shock to yourself or damage to your computer, do this before touching anything: ground yourself by placing two fingers gently on the metal case of your computer. This will drain any static charge.

Step 5: Locate the drive bay for your CD drive. Ground yourself again, then, holding the drive by the sides (not the front), insert it partway into the slot.

Step 6: Connect the audio output cable, power supply cable, and ribbon cable, then slide the drive the rest of the way in.
(For a detailed diagram showing these components, please see p. 16.)

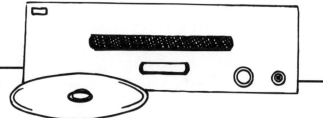

1. In what two steps do the instructions refer Darryl to another source for more detailed information? _____ , _____

2. Why do you think the writers of these instructions felt it necessary to include Step 2? _____

_____

_____

3. After reading Step 4, what do you think grounding is? _____

_____

_____

4. What do you think the screwdriver and pliers are for? _____

_____

5. Where can you go if you are not already familiar with connecting cables? _____

_____

6. Could you succeed in following these directions as is? Why or why not? _____

_____

Buyer beware! Some advertisers hope you *don't* read carefully. When it comes to ads, read every word carefully before you spend.

Directions: Some of the things you should watch for in ads are exaggerated claims, hidden costs, additional commitments, disclaimers, and exclusions. Find the "catch" in each ad below, and explain it on the line.

— THE INTERNET ACCESS YOU WANT! —

Switch to ISPerformance today for the newest online features like video chat. *Talk to anyone around the world!* Only $17.95 per month*. Just pop in the *free* disk and *go*!

For the first 100 min. $.99 per minute over 100; 2 year contract required.

1. What's the catch? _____

_____

_____

_____

_____

---

2. What's the catch? _____

_____

_____

_____

IMAGINE YOURSELF SURFING ON KAUAI OR LOUNGING ON A MAUI BEACH

SPEND A WEEK IN HAWAII *for only* $399!*

Includes 6 nights at the Hawaiian Hotel, free continental breakfast, and a rental car!

Hawaiian Hotel is on the island of Oahu. Price does not include airfare from the mainland or between islands.

YOUR SKIN CAN BE BLEMISH-FREE FOREVER!

Miracle Mask is an extraordinary breakthrough in fighting acne. It is so effective you'll see results overnight. Order today for only $39.95* plus $8.95 shipping and handling. You'll be glad you did!

for a 30-day supply. Your credit card will be billed this amount monthly.

3. What's the catch? _____

_____

_____

_____

_____

---

4. What's the catch? _____

_____

_____

_____

***Splash Water Park*
ANTI-SUMMER SPECIAL!**

School has started, but it's still warm. You can get in one more Splash before fall.

Save 50% off admission in September!*

**Half-price offer excludes weekends and holidays.*

Ever since you were a baby you've been on a schedule. Schedules are a big part of your life. Take the time to read them carefully.

Directions: The Warner family lives in a town that offers many city-sponsored classes and activities. The family sat down and looked at the schedules of things they were interested in. Read the schedules below and answer the questions.

Mrs. Warner—CERAMICS

Beginners Ceramics $25 material fee

Class	Day	Time	Instructor
C101	T Th	6-9 pm	Budling
C102	M W	5-8 pm	Budling
C103	Sat	12-3 pm	Braun

Intermediate Ceramics $25 material fee

Class	Day	Time	Instructor
C104	T Th	7-9 pm	Braun

Mr. Warner—GOLF

Improving Your Golf Game $10 material fee

Class	Day	Time	Instructor
G101	W F	7-8 pm	Lerner
G102	Sat	9-10 am	Aquinas
G103	Sat	1-2 pm	Lerner

Optional Video Study   free

Class	Day	Time	Instructor
G100	M	6-7 pm	Aquinas

Caroline Warner—JUDO

Introduction to Judo   requires proper clothing

Class	Day	Time	Instructor
J101 (girls)	M W	6-7 pm	Martin
J102 (boys)	M W	7-8 pm	Martin
J103 (co-ed)	Sat	10-11am	Lee

Advanced Judo requires proper clothing

Class	Day	Time	Instructor
J104 (adults)	Sat	9-10 am	Lee

1. Caroline, 13, has soccer practice on Saturday mornings. When is the only time she could take a Judo class?

   _____

2. Mr. Warner wants to take the Improving Your Golf Game class and the video study with the same instructor. What class should he take?

   _____

3. Mr. Warner has decided to take G102 and G100. If Caroline takes J101 in the building next door, on what day will they be in class at the same time?

   _____

4. Mrs. Warner does not get home from work on weekdays until 6 pm. What are her options for taking Ceramics?

   _____

5. Mrs. Warner took Beginners Ceramics last year and wants to improve her skills. Is there a class she can take that does not interfere with her work schedule?

   _____

6. The Warners want to set aside one weekday evening to spend together. If they each take the classes they want, what day are all three of them free?

   _____

Food is one of your basic needs. So is reading about it on container labels, menus, and in recipes.

Directions: Below are portions of the nutrition labels of two kinds of cereal: Honey Nuggets and Corny Crisps. Compare them and answer the questions.

A.

Nutrition Facts

Serving Size   1 cup
Servings Per Container about 11

Amount Per Serving	Cereal	Cereal with 1/2 cup Fat Free Milk
Calories	200	240
Calories from Fat 15		15
	% Daily Value	
Total Fat 1.5g	2%	2%
Saturated Fat 0g	0%	0%
Cholesterol 0mg	0%	0%
Sodium 70mg	3%	6%
Total Carbohydrate 16g	16%	16%
Dietary Fiber 4g	16%	16%
Sugars 12 g		

B.

Nutrition Facts

Serving Size   1 cup
Servings Per Container about 12

Amount Per Serving	Cereal	Cereal with 1/2 cup Fat Free Milk
Calories	100	140
Calories from Fat 0		0
	% Daily Value	
Total Fat 0g	0%	0%
Saturated Fat 0g	0%	0%
Cholesterol 0mg	0%	0%
Sodium 200mg	8%	11%
Total Carbohydrate 3g	4%	4%
Dietary Fiber 1g	4%	4%
Sugars 2 g		

1. Which cereal has more calories per serving? _____ more sodium? _____
   more fiber? _____

2. What does the addition of fat free milk add to a serving of either cereal? _____
   _____

3. Which cereal is the Honey Nuggets? _____ How can you tell? _____

4. Cereal B has six times as much _____ as Cereal A.

5. Both cereals show serving size as 1 cup. Is that realistic? _____

6. Do you think cereal is a good choice as part of a healthy breakfast? Why or why not?
   _____
   _____

7. Of these two cereals, which would you prefer to eat and why? _____
   _____

Directions: Eating out involves more than feeding your hunger. A restaurant menu gives you information such as food options, combinations, prices, and sometimes even the calorie count of your meal. Read the menu below and answer the questions.

Welcome to Ned's . . . Great Food Served With a Smile

SALADS

Plain House Salad—small	$1.75
large	$2.25
with chicken strips	$3.25

SANDWICHES

Burger with the works	$5.95
Chicken breast sandwich.	$5.49
BLT	$4.95
Tuna salad.	$4.95
Grilled cheese.	$4.49
w/ham	$4.95

SIDES

French fries	$1.19
Onion rings	$1.29
Fresh fruit salad	$1.59

ENTREES (includes veg. and a side)

1/2 Fried chicken.	$6.49
Salisbury steak	$6.49
Lasagna (meatless)	$5.49
Pork chops	$6.49
Macaroni and cheese	$4.49

DRINKS

Soda. . . . . $.89, $.99, $1.09
Milk (regular or fat-free)	$.79
Shake (choc. van. straw.)	$1.69
Coffee/tea	$1.25

DESSERTS

Ice cream (two scoops).	$2.25
Cookies (two, peanut butter).	$.89
Strawberry pie (in season)	$1.75

1. Paul wants a burger, fries, and a chocolate shake. He has $10. Is that enough? _____

2. Ted is a vegetarian. What entrees can he order? _____

_____

3. Marti ordered a tuna salad sandwich and a milk. She paid with a $20 bill. What change should she receive? _____

4. Telia is really hungry but watching her budget. What's the least expensive entree she can order? _____

5. What item on the menu will not always be available? _____

6. Renee loves bacon. What item on the menu would appeal to her? _____

7. Which costs more: a chicken breast sandwich and fries or a fried chicken entree?

_____

8. Dee and Tina decided to split a grilled cheese and a large soda.
   How much did each spend?_____

Directions: If you wanted to, you could make pizza from scratch. Read the recipe below to see how. Then answer the questions.

Make Some DOUGH

Yield: two 8" crusts; Recipe can be doubled and part frozen for use later.

Ingredients: 1¼ tsp. active dry yeast   ⅛ tsp. granulated sugar   ½ tsp. salt
(or one-half of ¼ oz. packet)   2 tbs. cornmeal   1¼ cup + 1 tbs. all-purpose
½ cup warm water   1 tsp. olive oil   flour (reserve tbs.)

Directions:

1. In a large bowl, sprinkle the yeast over the warm water, then stir in the sugar. Let it stand for about three minutes. It will appear foamy. Stir in cornmeal, salt, and oil.
2. Gradually add flour, stirring with a wooden spoon. Keep stirring until the dough becomes stiff and all the flour is mixed in well.
3. Dust a clean, flat surface with the reserved tablespoon of flour. Turn the dough onto the surface, then knead for about three minutes (until dough is smooth and stretchy).
4. Use non-stick cooking spray to coat the inside of a large bowl and place the dough in it. Cover it loosely with a moist towel or plastic wrap. Put the bowl in a warm, draft-free place, and let the dough rise until it is about double its original size. This will be about 90 minutes.
5. Punch the dough down. Form it into a ball and let it rise again for about 30 minutes.
6. Divide the dough in half with a knife. Use each half for one pizza crust.
7. Put the dough onto a floured surface. Roll it out until it is about 8" in diameter and about ⅛" thick.
8. Add whatever toppings you like and bake.

---

1. What do each of these abbreviations mean? tsp. _____ tbs. _____

2. What ingredient makes the dough rise? _____

3. What word in the recipe is a synonym for *damp*? _____

4. If you doubled the recipe, how much sugar would you need? _____

5. What word in the recipe means *set aside for later*? _____

6. What is the total amount of time the dough will be set aside to rise? _____

7. What does *knead* mean? _____

8. What word means *measurement across the center of a circle*? _____

9. Estimate about how long you think it would take to make pizza dough from start to finish? _____

Maybe some day the telephone will go the way of the pony express, but for now you still need to know how to find phone numbers for businesses and friends. One way is to use the Internet, but another way is with a printed phone book.

Directions: For this activity you will need a phone book with white pages and yellow pages (or one of each). If you don't have one they can be found in the library. Use it to answer the questions below. You may work alone or team up with a partner.

Phone Book

1. How are the listings in a phone directory organized?
   _____

2. What geographical area or area codes does your phone book cover? _____ How many pages does it have? _____

3. Look in the front of your phone book. Other than names and numbers, list three kinds of information your phone book offers. _____
   _____

4. Is your number listed in the book? If so, on what page? _____ If not, why not? _____

5. Where are the listings for government offices and services in your phone book? _____

6. Do the white pages of your phone book have separate listings for business and residential? _____

7. Does your yellow pages have an index? _____

8. Are the yellow pages alphabetized by business name or by category?
   _____

9. Which part of a phone book has advertising? _____

10. Find a locksmith service in your area.
    On what page did you find it? _____

    Does it provide 24-hour emergency service? _____

Everybody makes mistakes. Reading for errors is called proofreading, and takes special concentration and skill. Try it now.

Directions: Test your proofreading skills on the following flier. Look for mistakes in spelling, capitalization, punctuation, and usage. Identify the mistake in each numbered section. Write it correctly on the corresponding line.

❶ **GIANT SAIL!**

Come into

❷ **Sammys Sporting Goods Store**
Saturday and save!

❸ Sammy hisself will be in the store on Saturday from noon to five to hand out 10% off coupons.

❹ These savings will be applyed to our already low, low prices.

❺ Here's just a sample of the savings youll find:

❻ • **All athletic shoes for men and wemen 20% off!**

• **Buy any sweatshirt and get a second one free!**

• **Take $5 off any equipment priced at $50 or more.**

❼ Special hours in affect this Saturday only

8:00 am to 10:00 pm

Plenty of free parking

❽ **Sammy's Sporting Goods**

2348 w. newberry

Kensington, MI

❾ Don't be late! At these prices we can't guarantee we won't run out of what you want
Sorry, no rainchecks.

❶ _____

❷ _____

❸ _____

❹ _____

❺ _____

❻ _____

❼ _____

❽ _____

❾ _____

Scope and Sequence

Students

	prefixes, suffixes, root words	plurals/possessives	context clues	analogies	multiple meanings	synonyms/antonyms/homonyms	signal words	abbreviations	the five Ws	sequence	fact and opinion	classifying/categorizing	cause and effect	main ideas and details	drawing conclusions/inferences	compare/contrast	similes/metaphors/idioms	exaggeration	generalizations/summarization	preview and predict

Scope and Sequence

Students

	mapping story elements/events	mapping story characters	time reference/sequence	identifying tone/mood	identifying point of view	reading for a purpose	multiple comprehensive skills	alphabetical order	dictionary/glossary	table of contents/index	using a timeline	reading graphs	reading diagrams/tables	reading a map	following directions	advertising	schedules/labels	menus/recipes	using directions	proofreading

Common Core Skills & Strategies for Reading: Level 8

Answer Key

Page 2
1. 10	7. 4	13. ½
2. 5	8. 5	14. 8
3. 2	9. 2	15. 10
4. 3	10. 1,000	16. 4
5. 5	11. 1,000	
6. 8	12. 1	

Challengers:
every 200 years
70 (or in their 70s)

Page 3
1. nonfunctioning
2. triangle
3. bipolar
4. misunderstood
5. impatient
6. recycle
7. antiwar
8. multipurpose
9. preestablish
10. transpacific
11. subspace
12. transform
13. centimeter
14. nonagressive
15. resubmit
16. impersonal
17. multicultural
18. misinterpreted
19. tristate
20. predetermine

Page 4
1. hopeless
2. childhood
3. washable
4. violinist
5. northward
6. foolish
7. contentment
8. kindness
9. loyalty
10. fearful
11. teacher
12. psychology
13. wooden
14. duckling
15. strangely
16. worthless
17. golden
18. timely
19. fortyish
20. upward

Page 5
Prefix
reappear, undone,
misalign, discover,
impossible, immature,
nonsense, midnight
Suffix
poisonous, adulthood,
childish, wishful, chemist,
goodness, yellowish

Both
dishonesty, precooked,
nonworking, uninformed,
disagreement, recounted,
frequently
Neither
quite, appreciative

Page 6
1. not believable
2. having bends
3. move by hand
4. able to be heard
5. move to a new place
6. move into action
7. one who is on foot
8. speak against
9. a sudden break
10. below/outside the city
11. easy to see
12. pull toward
13. liked by people
14. break up or apart
15. make by hand
16. leave a place empty
17. a time to be heard
18. mach. moves by itself
19. seen with the eyes
20. the mark of identity

Page 7
1. asterisk, astronomy
2. cyclone, cyclical
3. autograph, graphic
4. telegram, diagram
5. diameter, thermometer
6. phonics, symphony
7. telephoto, photosynthesis
8. periscope, telescope
9. thermos, thermometer
10. biopsy, biology
11. geography, geology
12. hydroelectric, hydrant
13. optometrist, optical
14. phobia, claustrophobic

Page 8
	Prefix	Root	Suffix
1.		host	ess
2.	dis	comfort	
3.	re	define	
4.	im	port	
5.		annual	ly
6.	un	certain	ty
7.		thought	less
8.	mis	pronounce	
9.		govern	ment
10.		joy	ous
11.	ir	regular	
12.	anti	social	
13.	mis	lead	ing
14.	un	comfort	able
15.		sorrow	ful
16.		knight	hood
17.	sub	category	

18–20. Answers will vary.

Page 9
1. possess. 11. pl. possess.
2. pl. possess. 12. pl. possess.
3. plural 13. possess.
4. possess. 14. pl. possess.
5. possess. 15. possess.
6. plural 16. plural
7. possess. 17. possess.
8. plural 18. plural
9. plural 19. possess.
10. plural 20. plural

Page 10
1. in a secretive way
2. strongly wished for
3. vein of mineral ore
4. hold back; adversely...
5. necessities
6. stolen goods
7. vulnerable to attack
8. look alike; copy
9. newborn
10. destroy
11. members of cat family
12. in a positive way

Page 11
1. drudge	7. range
2. docent	8. declaration
3. copious	9. scowl
4. trifle	10. hospitable
5. reclined	11. palatable
6. donned	12. catatonic

Page 12
A. 1. acquiesced
2. adjudicate
3. agitated
4. ensued
5. adjacent
Description will vary.
B. 1. infuse
2. ichthyologist
3. hypothermia
4. aerated
5. contaminates
Description will vary.

Page 13
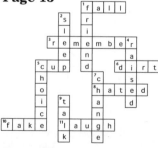

Page 14
Paragraph 1: disgruntled,
mutiny, technically
Paragraph 2: notoriety,
bolster, preceded, prior,
arrived

Paragraph 3: continents,
popular, construed, context
Paragraph 4: perspective,
previously, Obviously,
thriving

Page 15
A. 1. plants
2. flora
3. aesthetic
4. education/study
5. false
B. 1. fruit
2. regions
3. temperate
4. edible
5. false
C. 1. United States
2. era
3. a song
4. Texas
5. false

Page 16
1. speed up; make easier
2. similarity; resemblance
3. neither
4. riding equipment
5. comfort; cheer up
6. joy and celebration
7. heavily filled
8. having two equal-length
   sides
9. neither
10. parts in a series
11. convince; persuade
12. threat of force

Page 17
1. True	11. True
2. False	12. False
3. True	13. True
4. True	14. True
5. Unkn.	15. False
6. True	16. Unkn.
7. False	17. Unkn.
8. False	18. True
9. False	19. True
10. False	20. Unkn.

Page 18
Don—sundial
Lisa—supergiant
Tanya—sextant
Deion—pupil
Chris—Leonids
Pedro—luminescence
1. Lisa	4. Deion
2. Pedro	5. Chris
3. Tanya	6. Don

Notes: Answers will vary.

Page 19
Answers will vary.

Page 20
Answers will vary.

Page 21
1. Singular to Plural
2. Whole to Part
3. Part to Whole
4. Past to Present
5. Plural to Singular
6. Characteristics
7. Present to Past
8. Action to Object
9. Location
10. Object to Action
11. Sequence
12. Classification
13. Synonyms
14. Antonyms
15. Counterpart
Challenger:
16. roar
17. uncle
18. went
19. we're
20. most
21. exit

Page 22
A.	B.
1. plane	1. hop
2. icing	2. bell
3. blood	3. nose
4. bottle	4. paint
5. keys	5. beat
6. snake	6. sweep
7. fur	7. draw
8. corn	8. water
9. horse	9. nail
10. tree	10. door

May be other correct responses.

Page 23
size: 5, 16; shape: 3, 12, 18; color: 6, 9; sound: 1, 14, 20; smell: 7, 19; taste: 2, 15, 17; feel: 8, 11; composition: 4, 10, 13
1. loud
2. lemon
3. round
4. glass
5. tiny
6. grass
7. skunk
8. soft
9. yellow
10. tire
11. sandpaper
12. triangle
13. sweater
14. horse
15. pretzel
16. short
17. peach
18. jagged
19. basement
20. snake

May be other correct responses.

Page 24
1. drive
2. read
3. drink
4. eyes
5. type
6. wash
7. smell
8. dog
9. pot
10. hop
11. animals
12. watch
13. lungs
14. blow
15. shovel
16. refrigerator
17. fly
18. cut
19. feathers
20. fix

Page 25
C 1. finish
B 2. bear
D 3. head
A 4. fruit
B 5. moth
B 6. niece
C 7. dinner
D 8. classroom
A 9. doll
C 10. fifty
D 11. finger
A 12. bird

May be other correct responses.

Page 26
1. tale
2. different
3. leave
4. destroy
5. laugh
6. try
7. apart
8. stroll
9. needed
10. all
11. lead
12. hard

Page 27
Note: A1, B4, C3, D2
Park: E3, F1, G2, H2
Watch: I5, J4, K3, L2, M1, N6

Page 28
A) meaning: candy flavored with extract of a plant in that family
B) meaning: new or in its original form
C) meaning: a huge or unlimited amount or supply
D) meaning: a place where money is coined by authority of the government
E) meaning: any of various plants used for flavoring and aroma

Sentence answers will vary.

Page 29
Answers will vary.

Page 30
1. in a condition of
2. quarrel or squabble
3. moved very quickly
4. overtake; get to
5. stopped motionless
6. confront
7. mental stress
8. disapproving look
9. create; invent
10. became gentler
11. cow
12. Josh didn't get up on time.
13. She probably figured that he would miss the bus.
14. Josh's apology
15. wrong

Page 31
(1) bat (n) flying mammal
(2) bat (n) flutter
(3) bluff (n) steep cliff
(4) bluff (v) mislead; fool
(5) slip (n) thin piece
(6) slip (v) move easily
(7) hide (n) animal skin
(8) hide (v) conceal
(9) tire (v) grow weary
(10) tire (n) rubber wheel

Page 32
A.
1. grab, seize, nab, entrap
2. bond, attach, fasten
3. spew, scatter, disperse, diffuse
4. placid, serene, tranquil, still
5. devise, concoct, formulate
6. request, inquire, question
7. toil, work
8. sporadic, scarce, rare
B.
1. ill
2. swiftly
3. view
4. stalk
5. typically
6. victim
7. range
8. sprint
9. disperse
10. mere

Page 33
A.	B.
1. asked	1. strong
2. most	2. deep
3. change	3. empty
4. find	4. frown
5. allow	5. rise
6. destroy	6. shrink
7. uncertain	7. forget
8. something	8. wide
	9. noisy

Page 34

Page 35
1. amassed
2. ancient
3. keen
4. heavens
5. rapidly
6. ease
7. frequently
8. messenger
9. cognizant
10. obvious
Challenger: alias

Page 36
1. aloud
2. billed
3. dough
4. cellar
5. fur
6. clothes
7. border
8. site
9. corral
10. hangar
11. lead
12. lesson
13. mowed
14. sale
15. scent
16. leased
17. stationery

Page 37
1. peak; the summit…
2. patience; composure…
3. assistants; people…
4. whether; if
5. straight; directly…
6. peddle; sell
7. overdue; late
8. through; in and out…
9. vain; futile…
10. pause; a brief stop

Page 38
1. its
2. it's
3. its
4. its
5. its
6. your
7. your
8. you're
9. you're
10. your
11. who's
12. whose
13. who's
14. whose
15. who's
16. they're
17. they're
18. their
19. their
20. their

Page 39
A.
1. lose: misplace; not win
   loose: not tight
2. of: relating to
   off: not on; drop away…
3. than: compared with
   then: at that time…
4. affect: influence; cause
   effect: result; consequence
5. accept: agree to; take
   except: exclude; leave…
6. conscience: sense of…
   conscious: aware; awake
B. Correct as is: 2, 3, 7, 8, 10, 15. Incorrect: 1—except, 4—then, 5—lose, 6—accept, 9—effect, 11—then, 12—off, 13—loose, 14—than, 16—conscious

Page 40
1. a conclusion
2. an example or list
3. a conclusion
4. comparison/opposing idea
5. an example or list
6. more ideas will follow
7. comparison/opposing idea

8. comparison/opposing idea
9. a conclusion
10. comparison/opposing idea
11. comparison/opposing idea
12. an example or list
13. an important point
14. comparison/opposing idea
15. a conclusion

Page 41
1. Avenue
2. each
3. department
4. amount
5. Wednesday
6. Doctor
7. centimeter
8. quart
9. year
10. Governor
11. September
12. ounce
13. Mister
14. week
15. Road
16. December
17. Boulevard
18. dozen
19. Captain
20. Tuesday
21. gallon
22. Street
23. October
24. Mountain/Mount
25. Route
26. foot/feet
27. Friday
28. Junior
29. Highway
30. miles per hour
Challengers:
31. etc. 32. www 33. misc.

Page 42
1. Abraham Lincoln
2. Lincoln's assassination
3. Ford's Theater,
   Washington, D.C.
4. April 14, 1865
5. Wording will vary.
Challengers: wording will vary

Page 43
1. FANtastic Replicas, Inc.
2. a team jersey
3. by phone or online at
   www.anyfan.com
4. Aug. 31
5. to show your spirit
6. football fans
7. $49.95 + $5.95 s/h
8. in 7–10 days
9. to have in time for the
   season opener or the offer
   will expire

Page 44
Answers will vary.

Page 45
5, 6, X, 8, 3, 4, 2, 7, 1

Page 46
First row: 1, 3, 5
Second row: 6, 2, 4
1. Bend two pipe...
2. Hook the two...
3. Bend another...
4. Twist a fourth...
5. Make a head...
6. Glue the head...
Challenger: anwers will vary

Page 47
1. D   6. E
2. G   7. A
3. F   8. B
4. C   9. H
5. I
B. implement
   incredible
   mandate
   novelty
   nuisance
   rally
   recline
   shun
   smitten
Solution: prevalent

Page 48

Page 49
Numbers 3, 4, 7, and 10
are facts. The others are
opinions and either agree or
disagree may be marked.
Challenger: fun, cute,
important, easy, should,
enjoyable

Page 50
*Answers may vary if student
can justify. Suggested:*
A. But a healthy smile...
   It is hard work.
   You should visit...
   Brushing every day...
B. K-9 is a clever...
   Only the most...
   A police dog is...
   Both the officer and...
   Dogs are loyal...

Page 51
joy, pleasure: delighted,
amused, exuberant, gratified
fear, worry: apprehensive,
anxious, suspicious, uneasy
sadness: dejected, glum,
forlorn, despondent
love, caring: admiration,
considerate, affectionate,
devoted
ability, confidence: capable,
assured, effective, skillful
anger: hostile, aggravated,
irritated, enraged
Drawn expressions should
match emotions

Page 52
A. 750   J. 020
B. 290   K. 770
C. 170   L. 520
D. 910   M. 410
E. 880   N. 590
F. 390   O. 150
G. 660   P. 780
H. 340   Q. 630
I. 220

Page 53
1. D
2. C
3. no (class is mammal)
4. no
5. yes
6. A
7. 2
8. D
Challenger: bald eagle-C,
giant panda-A, hermit
crab-D, blue whale-B

Page 54
1. mother sent Jack to...
2. he traded for...
3. Jack was sent to bed...
4. she threw them...
5. he climbed the...
6. he was able to grab...
7. he chopped down...
8. he and his mother...

Page 55
*Answers will vary but must
show appropriate cause or effect.*

Page 56
A. detail, detail, main idea
B. main idea, detail, detail
C. detail, detail, main idea
D. detail, main idea, detail

Page 57
1. It must have been a very
   frightening experience.
2. The Real Value of Pompeii
   *(accept other answers if
   student can justify)*
3. no
4. The people carried them
   off to safety.
5. The excavation of Pompeii
   is of great historical
   importance.

Page 58
1. It was huge and ugly.
2. Out of Extinction
   *(accept other answers if
   student can justify)*
3. rough, net fishing,
   commotion
4. Southern
5. c.

Page 59
1. a
2. false
3. sympathy, guilt
4. taking responsibility
5. "We simply can't afford
   to add another one
   right now."

Page 60
1. An eclipse is named
   for the object that is
   hidden (or obscured).
2. the sun
3. the Earth
4. Answers will vary.
5. *any two:* and all that;
   got to talking; OK, I
   made that up; Hey;
   get it.

Page 61
*The following sentences
should be marked:*
Some spiders are...
The black widow is...
A spider can have...
*Remaining sentences should
be written out in paragraph
form.*

Page 62
I. Egypt is a nation...
   It covers an area...
   Most of the country...
   The Nile River...
II. The region that is...
   Great cities and ...
   The arid conditions...
   Great temples and...

Page 63
I. His Life
   A. Early Life
      1. Birth & Family
      2. Education
   B. Career
      1. As a Minister
      2. An an Orator
   C. Death
II. Impact of His Work
   A. During His Life
      1. Civil Rights
      2. Non-violent...
   B. After His Death
      1. Social Reform
      2. Continuation...
Answers will vary.

Page 64

A.
1. a.m.; She was waking up for school.
2. It had snowed.
3. It was just as she had hoped.

B.
1. parrot (or mynah bird); he can talk
2. precaution; sharp claws
3. routine; fit as a fiddle/See ya next year.

Page 65
1. Carlo's; same last name when married
2. They are twins.
3. No; He may have not gotten his license right away at 16.
4. Yes; Eighth graders can't drive.
5. Billy and Mark; Story says others go to school.
6. No; He picks them up.
7. Answer will vary.
8. No; He could be another kind of pet.

Page 66
1. A car salesman
2. A plumber
3. An architect
4. A bank teller
5. A social studies teacher
6. A museum curator
7. A forest ranger
8. A farmer
9. An ad designer
10. A house inspector

Page 67
A. 1. library
   2. overdue books
B. 1. zoo; yes
   2. monkeys or apes
C. 1. They would be traveling to the U.S.
   2. England

Page 68
1. move faster
2. in good physical condition
3. was confused; disoriented
4. decreased significantly
5. gotten taller quickly
6. valuable for sale at a good deal
7. in a difficult position; in trouble
8. laughing hard

Page 69
Answers will vary, but should demonstrate valid likenesses and differences.

Page 70
1. Both   7. Einstein
2. Edison   8. Both
3. Edison   9. Both
4. Both   10. Einstein
5. Neither   11. Both
6. Both

Page 71
Answers will vary.

Page 72
Similarities:
Spends most...in water
Has a long, sticky tongue
Goes through a tadpole...
Has smooth, moist skin
Is classified as...
Feeds mainly on insects
Begins life as an egg...
Moves in long leaps
Differences:
Has a long, sticky tongue
Goes through a tadpole...
Moves in short hops
Is classified as...
Has dry, bumpy skin
Feeds mainly on insects
Begins life as an egg...
Spends most...on land
Has stocky, compact body
Frogs vs. toads: Similarities

Page 73
A.
1. boomed like thunder
2. sparkled like diamonds
3. as quick as lightning
4. like a refrigerator
5. as old as the hills
B.
1. a real chicken
2. barked out
3. crawled along
4. buckets
5. a lemon

Page 74
1. get a kick out of
2. flew
3. raining cats and dogs
4. a green thumb
5. lend me a hand
6. eat my words
7. with an open mind
8. hit the books
9. pull the wool over my eyes
10. heavy
11. straighten up
12. hanging out
Wording of meanings will vary. Drawings will vary.

Page 75
Similes: like a bump on a log; like a hawk; as innocent as babies; as clear as day; as red as a beet
Metaphors: master artists; little prisoners; mountain of information
Idioms: rocks in my head; kept an eye on; pulling my leg; put my fears to rest; knocked me over with a feather; caught her attention; about to blast her; anger floated away

Page 76
A. mowed down a mile of trees; louder than a thunderstorm; fifty feet taller; mountain-size blue ox.
B. faster than lightning; drive with one blow; sparks flew from his hammers; weighed over twenty pounds; keep them from catching fire
C. could invent anything; which was really a snake thirty feet long; caught a cyclone; squeezed the rain out; rode it all the way to California; hit so hard it made a valley
Word choices will vary.

Page 77
A. 1. I think the task is..
   2. It was unusually...
   3. It was messy.
   4. It will take a long...
B. *Answers will vary.*

Page 78
A. 1. G   4. G
   2. S   5. S
   3. G   6. G
B. *Answer will vary. Suggested:*
The Greek's version of the constellations has survived for thousands of years.

Page 79
1. Valid   6. Valid
2. Valid   7. Invalid
3. Valid   8. Valid
4. Invalid   9. Valid
5. Invalid
Challenger: If the same person both wrote and illustrated children's books.

Page 80
1. Despite its latitude...
2. In summer north of...
3. Norway's lands...
4. Though further north...
5. Norway is a country...

Page 81
Answers may vary. Possibles are:
A.
1. shoreline, crust, barnacles, shellfish, attached, nuisance
2. barnacles
3. Barnacles are tiny shellfish that attach themselves permanently to surfaces. On ships, they can affect steering and machinery.
B. *Answers will vary.*

Page 82
Answers will vary.

Page 83
Answers will vary. Suggested:
1. opinion poll, methods, interviews, sample questionnaires, random
2. sentence #1
3. yes
4. yes
5. no
Paragraph should incorporate the adjustments as answered above.

Page 84
1. Fantasy
2. Mystery
3. Poetry
4. Historical Fiction
5. Biography
6. Realistic Fiction
7. Science Fiction
8. Folklore

Page 85
1. second person
2. first person
3. second person
4. third person
5. third person
6. Answers will vary

Page 86
Answers will vary but must show examples of first, second, and third person.

Page 87
Answers will vary but must include dictionary definitions.

Page 88
1. bona fide
2. au revoir
3. protege
4. modus operandi
5. laissez faire
6. vice versa
7. status quo

Page 89
Wording will vary.
1. prairie, summer 1847

2. family of pioneers
3. They stop by a stream for water and hear strangers approaching, and fear trouble.
4. The strangers were other friendly settlers.

Page 90

Dan (clockwise)
reading
Atlanta, Georgia
eighth
hopes to be a sports agent
baseball
honesty
saving money
Don (clockwise)
math
Seattle, Washington
eighth
wants to be a teacher
soccer
reliability
being tall

Page 91

Answers will vary.

Page 92

Bottom: *Answers will vary.*

Page 93

Answers will vary. Suggested:
...to roller blade with his friends.
...it's family day and he has to participate.
... museums and history will be boring.
...he's stalling; he really doesn't want to be there.
...intrigued.
...embarrassed/silly...that natural history could be interesting.

Page 94

Wording will vary.
1. A dog was heading home with his bone.
2. He crossed over a bridge.
3. He saw another dog with a juicy bone and wanted it, too.

4. He barked to scare off the other dog.
5. He dropped the bone he had into the water.
6. The dog ended up with no bones.

Page 95

Answers will vary.

Page 96

Wording will vary.
1. past; there's a log cabin and a doll made from cornhusks.
2. future; there's a pod, a capsule, and they are computer-guided to a distant planet, while in stasis.
3. present; Jenna is online using the Internet for research.
4. past; there's reference to war, the colonies, and a new nation, and they're using an inkwell.

Page 97

1. before
2. before
3. before
4. after
5. before
6. before
7. before
8. before
9. after
10 before
11. before
12. after
13. after
14. before

Page 98

1. eerie
2. nervous
3. comical
4. serious

Page 99

1. same, different, different
Wording will vary:
2. The first lets you know that it will be about being awake and the second about falling asleep fast.
3. The writer is very aware of time moving slowly; It lets the words flow and drift just like falling asleep.
4. spreading the type apart
5. irritated; frustrated; relaxed; comfortable

Page 100

1. narrator
2. author's experience OR fictional character

3. fictional character
4. fictional character
5. author's experience OR fictional character
6. narrator

Page 101

Answers must be written from the point of view of the character.

Page 102

Answers will vary.

Page 103

Answers will vary.

Page 104

A.
describe: to paint a...
instruct: to give direc....
inform: to share facts...
persuade: to convince
summarize: to explain...
entertain: to express...
B.
1. persuade
2. summarize
3. instruct
4. inform
5. describe
6. entertain

Page 105

1. to instruct
2. to entertain
3. to persuade
4. to describe
5. to inform
6. to instruct
7. to summarize
8. to describe
9. to persuade

Page 106

1. summarize
2. describe
3. persuade
4. instruct
5. inform
6. entertain
Puzzle Answer: a reason

Page 107

1. inform
2. phenomena
3. 350
4. Answer will vary.
5. four
6. Answer will vary.
7. Answer will vary.
8. nonfiction

Page 108

1. second person
2. monitor
3. Answer will vary.
4. Answer will vary.
5. #3; #2
6. immunizations
7. response

8. It's your job to provide for its needs.
9. non-fiction

Page 109

1. girl; spoken to by the name of Marsha.
2. first person
3. scanned like a hawk
4. compassionate
5. They don't think reptiles are lovable.
6. looked; trade
7. 3. hit on the edge
8. metaphor

Page 110

1. inform
2. 4 furlongs; 2640 ft.
3. the ship
4. Latin
5. kilometer
6. those that use the metric system
7. nautical
8. stature
9. as straight as a Roman mile
10. An air mile is slightly less distance OR about 796.1 feet
11. 5,280 feet
12. secured by tying; a measurement of speed over water
13. Answer will vary.

Page 111

1. A   6. F
2. H   7. G
3. B   8. I
4. C   9. J
5. E   10. D

Puzzle word order:
irksome
irrigate
legible
leisure
undaunted
unique
unscrupulous
unyielding
usable
usher
Puzzle answer: relinquish

Page 112

A.
1. An Apple for Miss..
2. Arrow to the Sun
3. The Cat in the Hat
4. A Christmas Carol
5. Jumanji
6. The Jungle Book
7. One Fine Day
8. A Visit to William...
9. Winnie-the-Pooh
10. A Wrinkle in Time

Common Core Skills & Strategies for Reading: Level 8

139

B.
1. Alcott, Louisa May
2. Cleary, Beverly
3. George, Jean C.
4. Goble, Paul
5. Konigsburg, E. L.
6. Sendak, Maurice
7. Udry, Janice May
8. van Allsburg, Chris
9. White, E. B.
10. Wilder, Laura Ingalls

Page 113

1. 975
2. after
3. 974
4. after
5. 975
6. before
7. 975
8. 974
9. after
10. 975
11. after
12. 974
13. before
14. 975
15. after
16. 974
17. before
18. 975
19. after
20. before

Page 114

1. carriage
2. eagle
3. esteem
4. friction
5. heart ·
6. humor
7. jolly
8. layer
9. nature
10. peak OR peek
11. quarter
12. rocket
13. socks
14. union

Page 115

Answers may vary depending on the dictionary used.
1. a web-footed South American rodent found in and around lakes and streams.
2. kwe zen OR kwi zen
3. a title, brief description, or key accompanying a map
4. Scottish: from pety meaning small
5. Doctor of Philosophy
6. let the buyer beware
7. in the South Pacific, west of Chile
8. on a building
9. sleeping
10. get
11. wear it
12. sky
13. hota
14. round
15. second OR lu'
16. Russian
17. f
18. yes

Bottom: Answers will vary.

Page 116

1. Both
2. Glossary B
3. Neither
4. Neither
5. Glossary A
6. Both
7. Glossary B
8. Both
9. Glossary B

Page 117

1. Chap. 1
2. pp. 9-12
3. no
4. p. 20
5. pp. 24-25
6. yes
7. p. 8
8. pp. 17-18
9. p. 16
10. granite, limestone, marble

Page 118

1. animals
2. alphabetical order
3. pp. 210-218
4. fish
5. no
6. sharks OR pp. 73-80
7. Answer will vary. (They are arthropods).
8. p. 32; will vary
9. snake
10. monkey; On the same page as spider monkey.

Page 119

1. 1962-1971
2. Surveyor 1
3. 1968
4. Apollo 11
5. 1962
6. Apollo 15
7. Wording will vary.

Page 120

1. 100 million
2. 20 million
3. 20th OR 1900-2000
4. 1920-1940
5. 1970
6. line graph
7. line graph
8. bar graph
9. 54 million

Page 121

1. O2, CO2, H2O
2. precipitation
3. carbon dioxide
4. absorption
5. absorb
6. water
7. rise
8. oxygen

9. Answers will vary.

Page 122

1. -19°
2. 20°, 35mph
3. 15°, 15 mph
4. 20°, 40 mph
5. -16°
6. 15°
7. 5°, 5 mph
8. Answer will vary.

Page 123

1. west
2. Pinewood Hospital
3. Rte. 71
4. south
5. left on Alpine, south to Pine Forest, turn left, proceed to Killian Way, then turn right.
6. no
7. Go north on Alpine to the entrance ramp on the right.

Page 124

Section 1: A. Filled in, all caps, last name first. B. birthdate in double digits. C. M or F D. grade E. date in double digits.
Section 2: written and circles filled in: 307295
Section 3: number filled in to match quarter
Section 4: left blank

Page 125

1. 3, 6
2. Answers will vary.
3. drain static charge
4. removing the cover of the computer
5. p. 16
6. Answer will vary.

Page 126

Answers will vary.

Page 127

1. M W 6-7 pm
2. G102, G100
3. Monday
4. Sat. 12-3 pm and T Th 7-9 pm.
5. yes; C103
6. Friday

Page 128

1. A, B, A
2. calories, sodium
3. A, added sugar
4. sugar
5–7. Answers will vary.

Page 129

1. yes
2. meatless lasagna or macaroni and cheese

3. $14.26
4. macaroni and cheese
5. strawberry pie
6. BLT
7. sandwich and fries
8. $3.29

Page 130

1. teaspoon, tablespoon
2. yeast
3. moist
4. 1/4 teaspoon
5. reserve
6. 120 min. OR 2 hrs.
7. repeatedly push with fists or hands
8. diameter
9. Answer will vary. (more than two hours. but less than three)

Page 131

1. alphabetical order
2–10. Answers will vary.

Page 132

1. sail / sale
2. Sammys / Sammy's
3. hisself / himself
4. applyed / applied
5. youll / you'll
6. wemen / women
7. affect / effect
8. w. newberry /W. Newberry
9. want   Sorry /want. Sorry